THE IMMORTALS: AN UNAUTHORIZED GUIDE TO SHERLOCK AND ELEMENTARY

by

Matthew J Elliott

First edition published in 2013
© Copyright 2013
Matthew Elliott

The right of Matthew Elliott to be identified as the author of this work has been asserted by him in accordance with the Copyright, Designs and Patents Act 1998.

All rights reserved. No reproduction, copy or transmission of this publication may be made without express prior written permission. No paragraph of this publication may be reproduced, copied or transmitted except with express prior written permission or in accordance with the provisions of the Copyright Act 1956 (as amended). Any person who commits any unauthorised act in relation to this publication may be liable to criminal prosecution and civil claims for damage.

The opinions expressed herein are those of the authors and not of MX Publishing.

Paperback ISBN 9781780924908
ePub ISBN 9781780924915
PDF ISBN 9781780924922

Published in the UK by MX Publishing
335 Princess Park Manor, Royal Drive,
London, N11 3GX
www.mxpublishing.com

Cover design by www.staunch.com

"Sherlock Holmes, the immortal character of fiction created by Sir Arthur Conan Doyle, is ageless, invincible and unchanging. In solving significant problems of the present day he remains – as ever – the supreme master of deductive reasoning."

Onscreen introduction to *Sherlock Holmes and the Voice of Terror*, *Sherlock Holmes in Washington* and *Sherlock Holmes and the Secret Weapon*

"I love *Elementary* and *Sherlock* both. I think they are terrific, fresh interpretations."

Leslie S Klinger

This book would not have been possible without the extraordinary vision of Steve Emecz, the invaluable input of Luke Benjamen Kuhns, Bonnie MacBird, Roger Johnson, Ian Potter, Jim French and Larry Albert, and the patience of my wife Gill.

Contents

Part One: Every Good Little Boy and Girl Looks Forward to Present Day……………………………..3

Sherlock Season One……………………………………9

Sherlock Season Two…………………………………..48

Part Two: Sherlock Holmes in New York…………….85

Elementary………………………………………..91

Part One: Every Good Little Boy and Girl Looks Forward to Present Day

This is the last time I tell this story...

It's Friday, 23rd July 2010, and I get an e-mail from the producers of *Newsnight*. This makes a pleasant change from my usual communications from down-on-their-luck members of the Nigerian Royal Family, so I'm eager to read it. In my position as host of the Sherlock Holmes Society of London's annual film evening, it seems I'm considered an expert of some sort, and I didn't even have to sit a test in order to gain this qualification (just as well, I tend to fold under pressure). There's a new Sherlock Holmes series starting on BBC 1 on Sunday night, and would I like to be interviewed in the London studio alongside writer/co-creator/producer Steven Moffat? I decide very quickly that, yes, that might be quite nice.

"Your postcode, where is that?" the researcher asks.

"Wigan," I say. "I'm near Manchester."

"Ohhhh..."

"Problem?"

Yes, there is a problem. Getting me from Manchester to London involves paying my train fare, and then I'd have to stay overnight, which means a hotel bill...

"Thanks, but we've decided to go another way with the interview."

So that was that, the closest I got to *Sherlock*. I'm totally over it now. Now, let's get bang up to date – which requires us to go back to 1939. Sorry about that.

In 1939, Basil Rathbone and Nigel Bruce were teamed together for the first time in 20th Century Fox's adaptation of *The Hound of the Baskervilles*. The casting was revolutionary, the production lavish. A sequel, *The Adventures of Sherlock Holmes*, followed that same year.

In 1942, the series moved to Universal. Rathbone and Bruce were still together, but there was one significant change – the series now took place not in the 19th Century, but in the present day. Holmes and Watson were living in a world of automobiles, wirelesses and Nazis. Unthinkable! So radical was the notion that Universal felt obliged to preface the first three movies in the series with an almost apologetic message that stressed the immortal nature of the character of Sherlock Holmes, echoing the sentiments of Orson Welles in the introduction to his 1938 radio adaptation of William Gillette's stage play: "(He is) a gentleman who never lived and will never die."

But why apologize at all? Sherlock Holmes has been depicted on film almost as long as there's been film. The 1939 *Hound of the Baskervilles* is by no means the first Holmes film – it's not even the first *Hound of the Baskervilles* film. But every movie prior to Rathbone's début, including entire series featuring silent-era actor Eille Norwood and uncanny Holmes lookalike Arthur Wontner, were set in the present, whatever the present happened to be at that time. The decision to put Holmes in period was truly revolutionary, as was the casting of Rathbone himself, who was a match for the famous Sidney Paget illustrations in the *Strand* magazine, but not for the American notion of Holmes, drawn from the work of artist Frederic Dorr Steele, which were in turn based on the visage of aforementioned stage actor William Gillette. Most American movie Holmeses prior to Rathbone tended towards the chunky. But so powerful was the image of Holmes and Watson in a gas-lit London that to attempt to move him on in time after that would require a damn good explanation.

After the final Rathbone/Bruce movie in 1946, Holmes would only be brought into the present day by means of a science fiction gimmick (*The Return of Sherlock Holmes* in 1987 and *Sherlock Holmes Returns* in 1993) or for the purposes of attempted comedy – John Cleese, I'm looking at you.

That Sherlock Holmes found his way into the 21st Century is due in no small part to Russell T Davies' phenomenally successful reinvention of *Doctor Who*. Long before taking the creative reins of the show, Steven Moffat scripted the celebrated two-parter *The Empty Child* for the first series of the revival. Mark Gatiss, co-creator of *Sherlock* penned *The Unquiet Dead* for that same season, and on their train journeys to Cardiff, the notion of a modern day Sherlock Holmes and Dr Watson was first discussed. As a side note, it's interesting that many *Doctor Who* fans are also Sherlock Holmes fans. I'm not sure it's the case, however, that all Holmes fans are necessarily *Who* fans. I don't know whether that's a subject worthy of further investigation, but if I had to guess, I'd say it probably isn't.

Firm plans for a series were made at an awards ceremony in Monte Carlo (story of my life, too) and a sixty-minute episode was filmed in 2009, with Benedict Cumberbatch and Martin Freeman in the lead roles. So positive was the response at the BBC that a series of ninety-minute episodes were ordered, necessitating a complete remount of that first story. Certain newspapers were quick to claim, based on no evidence whatsoever, that the pilot episode was so terrible it had been decided that it must never be seen – it can, by the way, be seen on the DVD of *Sherlock* Season One.

It's an odd thing, but Sherlock Holmes never really goes away. Lord Peter Wimsey hasn't been seen on our screens since 1987, but Holmes crops up with astonishing regularity – by the time the first episode of *Sherlock* aired, the character had already made a triumphant return to the big screen, as played by Robert Downey Jr in Guy Richie's

Pirates of the Caribbean-esque blockbuster. The BBC itself hadn't given up on Holmes, either. In the eight years prior to the first episode of *Sherlock*, there were three separate productions based on the character, beginning with an adaptation of *The Hound of the Baskervilles* in 2002, starring Richard Roxburgh and Ian Hart. Hart returned as Watson opposite Rupert Everett in 2004's clumsily-titled *Sherlock Holmes and the Case of the Silk Stocking* (filmed as *The Return of Sherlock Holmes* and later publicised as *Sherlock Holmes and the Deadly Season*). Jonathan Pryce and Bill Paterson took the leads in the children's miniseries *Sherlock Holmes and the Baker Street Irregulars*, just two years before the filming of the pilot episode of *Sherlock*.

Hopefully, there'll be time to look at these other productions in depth another day, but this volume focuses upon the two modern day television series, the BBC's *Sherlock* in the UK, and *Elementary* on CBS in the States. In order to consider each episode properly, I've broken them down into their component parts, each one prefaced with a quote from the works of Conan Doyle.

The best and the wisest man: Holmes' notable moments in this episode.

I am lost without my Boswell: Watson's notable moments in this episode.

The efficiency of our detective police force: The notable moments of the police regulars in this episode.

There is a strong family resemblance about misdeeds: Identification of material drawn from the Canon (and sometimes from other sources).

I have never loved: Sex and romantic relationships.

A seven-per-cent solution: Drug references.

A certain unexpected vein of pawky humour: Comedic moments.

My head is in a whirl: Logical inconsistencies within the episode.

It goes without saying that this book **CONTAINS SPOILERS**. In fact, I might go so far as to say that this book is one massive spoiler. If you haven't seen either of these series, and you don't want the plotlines ruined for you, I advise you to watch both of them before reading any further.
 Watched them all? Good. Hi, welcome back. Fun, wasn't it? I don't know about you, but I especially liked the one with the aluminium crutch. Now, if you'd care to join me, the game is afoot once more.

SHERLOCK
BBC

Co-created by Steven Moffat & Mark Gatiss

Executive Producers: Steven Moffat, Mark Gatiss, Beryl Vertue & Sue Vertue

Music: David Arnold & Michael Price

Regular Cast: Benedict Cumberbatch (Sherlock Holmes); Martin Freeman (Dr John Hamish Watson); Una Stubbs (Mrs Hudson); Rupert Graves (DI Greg Lestrade); Louise Brealey (Molly Hooper); Mark Gatiss (Mycroft Holmes); Andrew Scott (Jim Moriarty); Vinette Robinson (Sgt Sally Donovan); Tanya Moody (Ella); Jonathan Aris (Anderson); Zoe Telford (Sarah Sawyer)

Mark Gatiss and Rupert Graves do not appear in *The Blind Banker*. Gatiss does not receive a credit in Season One (since to do so would ruin the revelation at the end of *A Study in Pink* that he is not, in fact, Moriarty).
Louise Brealey does not appear in *The Hounds of Baskerville*.
Andrew Scott appears in *The Great Game* in Season One and throughout Season Two.
Vinette Robinson appears in *A Study in Pink*, *The Great Game* and *The Reichenbach Fall*.
Tanya Moody appears in *A Study in Pink* and *The Reichenbach Fall*.
Jonathan Aris appears in *A Study in Pink* and *The Reichenbach Fall*.
Zoe Telford appears in *The Blind Banker* and *The Great Game*.

Season One

1X01: A Study in Pink
UK Airdate: 25 July 2010

Writer: Steven Moffat
Director: Paul McGuigan

Guest Cast: Siobhán Hewlett (Helen); William Scott-Mason (Sir Jeffrey Patterson); Victoria Wicks (Margaret Patterson); Sean Young (Gary); James Duncan (Jimmy); Ruth Everett (Political Aide); Syrus Lowe (Political Aide); Katy Maw (Beth Davenport); Ben Green (Reporter); Pradeep Jey (Reporter); Imogen Slaughter (Reporter); David Nellist (Mike Stamford); Louise Breckon-Richards (Jennifer Wilson); Jonathan Aris (Anderson); Lisa Mcallister (Anthea); Stanley Townsend (Angelo); Peter Brooke (Taxi Passenger); Phil Davis (Jeff); Lasco Atkins (Late Night Pedestrian)*; Alison Egan (Jimmy's Mum)*

*Uncredited

Plot: Former army surgeon John Watson is finding it hard to come to terms with civilian life, plagued as he is by memories of his tour of duty in Afghanistan. His therapist Ella encourages him to write a blog, but Watson insists that nothing worth writing about ever happens to him. He's largely oblivious to the bizarre series of suicides plaguing London and dismaying Detective Inspector Lestrade. All three victims have voluntarily taken the same poison, but there are no clear connections between them.

Watson bumps into his old friend and colleague Mike Stamford. Over a cup of coffee, Stamford mentions an acquaintance who, like Watson, happens to be looking for someone to share the expense of a flat. John is first introduced to Sherlock Holmes in the lab at St Bartholomew's Hospital. Sherlock has his eye on an address on Baker Street, no.221B, just above Speedy's Sandwich Bar and Café.

As they are in the process of moving in, Sherlock is visited by Inspector Lestrade – another suicide has been discovered in an abandoned house in Brixton. The victim is a woman named Jennifer Wilson, who in life favoured an alarming shade of pink. For some reason, she scratched the letters R-A-C-H-E into the floorboards as she died. Sherlock deduces that she came from Cardiff, and possessed a suitcase. But the case is missing. Excited, he rushes off.

John is left to walk home alone. He receives a sinister call from a mysterious individual instructing him to get into a waiting car. He's driven to a warehouse where he is questioned by the same urbane gentlemen who spoke to him on the telephone. The gentleman describes himself as Sherlock's arch-enemy, and offers John money to keep an eye on his new flatmate. John flatly refuses.

Returning to Baker Street, Sherlock asks John to send a text to Jennifer Wilson's missing phone suggesting that she's still alive and requesting a meeting with the recipient on Northumberland Street. The detective has found Jennifer Wilson's case – the killer dumped it once he realised it was still in his vehicle, but Sherlock believes its probable that he still has the phone.

Staking out the Northumberland Street address from the Italian restaurant opposite, they see a taxi pull up at the kerb. Before they can question the passenger, the vehicle sets off again. Sherlock and John chase after the cab on-foot, and are eventually able to catch up with it. But the fare is a Californian tourist who has never been in London before – clearly, then, the cab was simply slowing down, and has nothing whatever to do with the crime.

They come home to find their Baker Street rooms being searched by Lestrade's officers. The Inspector has grown tired of Sherlock acting on his own, and demands his co-operation. Rachel, it seems, is the name of Jennifer Wilson's stillborn daughter. Sherlock realises that "Rachel" is also the password of her mobile phone, which can be tracked by GPS – she deliberately planted her phone on her killer. When John logs into Jennifer's account, the phone appears to be within 221B Baker Street. As Lestrade's officers search for the phone, a cab driver arrives to pick up Sherlock. He is the one one with the phone, the killer who stalks the streets of London unnoticed.

Leaving John and his house guests, Sherlock goes with the driver, Jeff, who has picked out another secluded spot for his victim, the deserted Roland-Kerr Further Education College. Jeff presents Sherlock with two bottles, each containing a pill; one is poisoned, the other harmless. Sherlock must pick one, and Jeff will take the other – the offer he made to all his victims. Sherlock correctly deduces that Jeff is dying of an aneurysm, but he is surprised to know that his serial killer adversary has a sponsor, who provides money to Jeff's children for each crime successfully committed.

Troubled after the police have abandoned the search, John decides to track the phone, and, by extension, Sherlock and the killer. But when he arrives at the college, he picks the wrong building. He's at the window opposite just as Sherlock and Jeff are about to take their pills – he shoots Jeff and brings an end to the challenge. In the killer's final moments, he gives Sherlock the name of his sponsor: "Moriarty."

Sherlock realises that John is the man responsible for saving his life, but doesn't tell Lestrade in order to prevent his friend suffering any legal reprisals. As they leave the crime scene, they are confronted by the man who waylaid John earlier in the evening; he's not Moriarty, but Sherlock's elder brother Mycroft. He'll be keeping a close eye on them from now on.

The best and the wisest man: Sherlock Holmes prefers to text rather than use a landline. He is owed a favour by Mrs Hudson, which comes in the form of a rent reduction after he took the trouble to ensure that her husband was executed in Florida. He keeps a skull, which he refers to as a friend (just as *Elementary*'s Holmes owns a phrenology bust named Angus). He finds he thinks better when he talks aloud, and until John's appearance, the skull has served as his companion and sounding-board (it does, after all, have the grand gift of silence) – Mrs Hudson takes it away, though it appears in later episodes, serving as the hiding place for Sherlock's emergency stash of cigarettes in *The Hounds of Baskerville*. He refuses to wear the traditional crime scene onesies, although he does so in the pilot version. He has more than one enemy. Now and then, people assume he's guilty of the crimes he investigates. He picks Lestrade's pockets whenever he finds the policeman annoying (and therefore has a fine collection of ID cards belonging to Scotland Yard's silver fox, and, we learn in Season Two, one belonging to Mycroft). He's placed a pair of eyes in the microwave as part of an experiment – good thing John didn't need anything defrosting in a hurry. When Anderson calls him a psychopath, he states that he is, in fact, "a high-functioning sociopath." Once he's proven that Jeff's gun is a fake, there's absolutely nothing to stop him from walking away, but he just can't bear to leave without knowing whether or not he has chosen the right pill – his addiction to danger is as powerful as John's, especially if it results in him being acknowledged as smarter than his adversary. He's not above torturing the dying Jeff to get Moriarty's name (that sequence recalling Harry Callahan's treatment of the killer Scorpio in the original *Dirty Harry*).

I am lost without my Boswell: It's perhaps fitting that, as the actor who portrayed Arthur Dent in the big-screen version of *The Hitch Hikers Guide to the Galaxy*, Freeman's John Watson is first seen in his pyjamas. Watson has kept his army revolver – it's in an unlocked drawer in his flat, under his laptop. The potential risks in doing this hardly need pointing out – the laptop could get very badly scratched. He hasn't written a word of his blog. He can read upside-down writing, and finds it difficult to trust (did someone let him down in a combat situation?). He considers himself very good at his job, although his observations at the crime scene aren't particularly insightful. His therapist believes his limp is psychosomatic, and Sherlock agrees with her – in the opening scene, his stick is across the room from his bed, the implication being that he doesn't really need it. He eventually leaves it in Angelo's restaurant when pursuing Jeff's cab, his limp forgotten in the excitement of the chase. He has in intermittent tremor in his left hand, which his therapist diagnoses as post-traumatic stress disorder. In fact, it's just the opposite - once he's under stress, the tremor stops. Despite the fact that he's just been kidnapped, he feels confident enough to attempt to chat up Mycroft's glamorous assistant Anthea. Freeman doesn't sport the traditional Watsonian moustache. In fact, the famous upper lip adornment is the invention of *Strand* Magazine artist Sidney Paget – Conan Doyle doesn't mention it until *The Naval Treaty* in the second short story collection, *The Memoirs of Sherlock Holmes*. Trailers suggest that Freeman will sport the facial fungus briefly in

Season Three. In the pilot, Watson throws away his gun to avoid prosecution, but that's not the case here – he threatens the Golem with it in *The Great Game*, and in Sherlock's hands it forms the basis of the season's cliffhanger. The exact location of Watson's war wound has been the subject of some debate among scholars. In *A Study in Scarlet*, he writes that he was "struck on the shoulder by a Jezail bullet, which shattered the bone and grazed the subclavian artery." But in the second novel, *The Sign of Four*, Holmes questions whether his friend's leg will stand a long trek in pursuit of the villain. Here, it's explained that John's was indeed wounded in the shoulder and that his limp is psychosomatic. Incidentally, Robert Duvall was the first actor to portray Watson with a limp, in the 1976 film *The Seven-Per-Cent Solution*. In the Robert Downey Jr series, Jude Law is seen to limp from time-to-time depending on whether or not someone reminds him.

The efficiency of our detective police force: Lestrade is played by the George Clooney-esque Rupert Graves, a far cry from Conan Doyle's description of the character as a "little sallow, rat-faced, dark-eyed fellow." His name is pronounced either "Lestrayde" or "Lestrarde" depending upon the adaptation (supposedly, Conan Doyle intended it to be the former). Here, it's "Lestrarde," as it is in the Basil Rathbone series. His first initial is G in the books – in *The Hounds of Baskerville*, we find out that his name is Greg. The Inspector knows enough about Sherlock's history to expect to find drugs at 221B. Like his consultant, he wears a nicotine patch – just the one, though, it's not like he's addicted to them. He and Sherlock have known each other for five years. He believes the detective to be a great man, and hopes that one day he might be a good one, also.

Sergeant Sally Donovan is in charge of the press conference regarding the suicides. She addresses Sherlock as "freak." She warns John that one day Sherlock will be responsible for the crime he's investigating (a prediction she has reason to believe has come true in *The Reichenbach Fall*).

The forensics officer on the case is Anderson, who refuses to work with Holmes. Despite possessing David Mitchell's voice and the worst haircut in London, Anderson is apparently having an affair with Sally Donovan; either that, or his floors really *did* need a good scrubbing. It's a measure of Sherlock's popularity that there's no shortage of volunteers when Lestrade wants the Baker Street rooms searched.

There is a strong family resemblance about misdeeds: The plot is based surprisingly closely on the first Sherlock Holmes novel, *A Study in Scarlet*, originally published in 1887. Many lines of dialogue from Conan Doyle's story appear verbatim in the episode. The significant difference, apart from the obvious move from the 19th to the 21st Century, is the fact that in the novel the killer is seeking vengeance on two specific victims, rather than outliving the healthy, largely out of spite. In Conan Doyle's original, American Jefferson Hope – who, like his counterpart, Jeff (who isn't actually named onscreen), is slowly dying from an aneurysm – hails from America, and his sole intention is to do away with his enemies by means of a fast-acting poison (although the second victim refuses to take it and is stabbed instead). Watson and Stamford drink from coffee cups labelled "Criterion" - in the novel, they have a chance encounter at the Criterion Bar. Holmes is first seen beating a cadaver with a riding crop, in order to ascertain what bruises form over the course of 20 minutes. He correctly deduces that Watson has been in Afghanistan. The clue regarding the message "Rache" is reversed for this story. It isn't written by the killer, but the victim, and isn't intended to be the German for "Revenge," which, in the novel, it is.

Sherlock and John's landlady is a Mrs Hudson – she points out that she's not a housekeeper, though she acts like it. Apparently, she has a hip. Mrs Hudson is mentioned in many stories, though she only really plays a significant part in *The Empty House* and *The Dying Detective*. Her first name is never given, but many assume it to be Martha, the name given to "the pleasant old lady" who assists Holmes in his capture of the German spy Von Bork, in the World War I adventure *His Last Bow*. In this episode, Mrs Hudson mentions a Mrs Turner next door, who is landlady to a married gay couple. In *A Scandal in Bohemia*, Conan Doyle briefly forgot the name he assigned to the landlady and had Holmes refer to her as "Mrs Turner." This was not his only lapse, however – in *The Man With the Twisted Lip*, Watson is called James instead of John (see *A Scandal in Belgravia* for more on this), and when the policeman from *The Sign of Four* reappears in *The Red-Headed League* his name has changed from Athelney Jones to Peter Jones.

Steven Moffat skilfully works in references to other Canonical adventures. The second victim is named James Phillimore, who meets his fate after returning home for his umbrella. In *The Problem of Thor Bridge*, Watson lists several of Holmes' unsolved cases, including that of "Mr James Phillimore, who, stepping back into his own house to get his umbrella, was never more seen in this world." Watson complains in *The Musgrave Ritual* that Holmes is in the habit of keeping his unanswered correspondence transfixed by a jack-knife into the very centre of of his wooden mantelpiece. Here, Sherlock is seen to embed a knife in the fireplace. His website is called *The Science of Deduction*, and seems to play the same role his magazine article *The Book of Life* did in the original. *The Science of*

Deduction is the title of the second chapter of *A Study in Scarlet* and the first chapter of *The Sign of Four*. When Holmes is consulted about the body in Lauriston Gardens, he declares: "the game, Mrs Hudson, is on!" a variation upon the oft-quoted "the game is afoot!", Holmes' declaration in only one story, *The Abbey Grange*, itself drawn from Shakespeare's *Henry V*. The deductions relating to John's phone are very similar to the ones made by Holmes in *The Sign of Four* concerning the pocket watch formerly owned by Watson's dipsomaniac brother. In this instance, however, Sherlock is slightly wrong – Harry isn't John's brother, but his sister.

Watson's shooting of the villain at the story's climax is somewhat similar to Sebastian Moran's attempt on Holmes' life in *The Empty House* – even more so in the pilot episode.

The text John receives from Sherlock - "Come at once, if convenient; if inconvenient, come anyway" - is almost identical to the message Holmes sends in *The Creeping Man*. His conversation with Italian restaurant owner Angelo is taken almost verbatim not from any Canonical source, but from the final Basil Rathbone/Nigel Bruce movie, *Dressed to Kill* (AKA *Sherlock Holmes and the Secret Code*, AKA *Prelude to Murder*). Good thing it's in the public domain, too.

One of the waiters at Angelo's restaurant is named Billy. Given the sheer mass of Canonical references in this episode, it's probably not a stretch to suggest that he's named after the Baker Street page boy, who is first identified in the final Holmes novel, *The Valley of Fear*. Billy is a creation of actor William Gillette, who included the character in his 1899 stage play. There's another Billy in *The Hounds of Baskerville* – he's the cook at the Cross Keys Inn, but that probably *is* just coincidence.

The "three-patch problem" is a play on the "three-pipe

problem" of *The Red-Headed League*. Holmes is famous for smoking, of course - not solely pipes, but let's be honest, mainly pipes. The Sherlock of, um, *Sherlock*, doesn't smoke, but only because modern social constraints have made it impossible (unless you're outdoors, of course).

Sherlock's elder brother Mycroft also appears, a further embellishment upon the plot of the original pilot. Mycroft appears in only two stories, *The Greek Interpreter* and *The Bruce-Partington Plans*. He's seven years older than Sherlock in the Canon, but it isn't confirmed in the BBC series that Mycroft is the elder of the two until *A Scandal in Belgravia*. His influential role in the British Government is established in the latter story. His main qualities are his idleness and his size; Conan Doyle describes him as "absolutely corpulent." Of course, had producers of *Sherlock* cast an absolutely corpulent actor in the role, it would've been instantly obvious to the initiated that Big Brother is watching John, and the fellow who attempts to bribe him is not, therefore, Moriarty. In the final scene, Sherlock makes a gibe about his brother "putting on weight," though Mycroft insists he's actually losing it - this is the age of liposuction, after all. There's a mention of his diet in the final episode of this season, *The Great Game*. Oddly, there have been more thin onscreen Mycrofts than fat ones, including Christopher Lee in Billy Wilder's *The Private Life of Sherlock Holmes* (1970) and Richard E Grant in *A Case of Evil* (2002). Here, he's played by *Sherlock*'s co-creator Mark Gatiss, who dyes his hair for the role. The makers of *Elementary* have cast their own slimline Mycroft, Welsh actor Rhys Ifans, for Season Two.

The offer of money to keep an eye on Sherlock made by the mysterious figure who might be Moriarty, but actually turns out to be Mycroft, suggests David Stuart Davies' pastiche novel *The Veiled Detective*, in which Watson is in Moriarty's employ.

The disdain with which Mark Gatiss utters the letter "B" in John's new address is a deliberate homage to Charles Kay's delivery in the 1991 adaptation of *The Creeping Man*, starring Jeremy Brett.

I have never loved: John spends much of the episode insisting that he and Sherlock are not gay (Martin Freeman's deadpan comic skills get a good workout in these sequences, so file this under **A certain unexpected vein of pawky humour**, too). Mrs Hudson assumes they'll be sharing the same bedroom. At the Italian restaurant, Angelo (who looks as though he should be comedian Bill Bailey, but isn't) places a candle on Sherlock and John's table to make things more romantic. During their conversation, Sherlock says that girlfriends are "not really his area" (he's utterly oblivious to Molly Hooper's attempts to win his affections at Bart's). When questioned about boyfriends, he mistakenly thinks John is trying to chat him up. "I think you should know that I consider myself married to my work, and while I'm flattered by your interest..."

A seven-per-cent solution: Sherlock appears to be in the throes of a drug-induced euphoria as John returns to their Baker Street rooms. In fact, he's wearing nicotine patches. "Impossible to sustain a smoking habit in London these days," he complains. John finds the idea that Sherlock might take drugs laughable. His flatmate is less amused.

A certain unexpected vein of pawky humour: John returns to Baker Street in response to a summons from Sherlock, who just wants to use his phone, and didn't like disturbing Mrs Hudson.

Sherlock: "Shut up." Lestrade: "I didn't say anything." Sherlock: "You were thinking. It's annoying."

A nice visual gag: there's a completed Rubik's Cube in the flat at Baker Street.

John: "Why didn't I think of that?" Sherlock: "Because you're an idiot. No, don't look like that. Practically everyone is."

John: "So I'm basically filling in for your skull?" Sherlock: "Relax, you're doing fine."

Sherlock: "If you were dying, if you'd been murdered, in your very last few seconds, what would you say?" John: "Please, God, let me live."

Sherlock: "Anderson, don't talk; you lower the IQ of the entire street."

My head is in a whirl: It takes a surprisingly long time for Sherlock to work out just how the killer can be invisible and in plain sight simultaneously, almost as though the writer had been forced to add an extra half an hour to the episode.

You'd think that a thorough search of Baker Street by a team of police officers would turn up all of Lestrade's missing ID cards, but no.

It's bizarre that the coppers should simply leave Baker Street and forget all about the phone just because its location has altered. Wouldn't that be a reason for chasing after it, especially if, as Donovan and Anderson are both convinced, Sherlock has it because he's the killer?

Why, exactly, is Moriarty sponsoring Jeff? There's no financial gain in it for him. Does he keep a file of projects listed "Shits & Giggles"?

"Is it nice not being me? It must be so relaxing." After three failed attempts to bring Sherlock Holmes back to our television screens, the BBC finally hits upon a successful formula, one that proves how little Conan Doyle's works have dated in the last 130 years. A pacey plot, sparkling script (a brilliantly-constructed patchwork quilt of references) and endearing performances all combine to make *Sherlock* an instant hit, in spite of the series' lack of pre-publicity. The most notable and original feature is the unique visual element – the projection onto the screen of both Sherlock's thought-processes and the many texts sent and received during the course of the series. The cab chase is accompanied by maps and road signs as he works out the best route by which to pursue his quarry. The music within the episode itself – different from that used in the one-hour pilot version - is seemingly inspired by the gypsy melodies in the Oscar-nominated score for Robert Downey Jr's film, as composed by Hans Zimmer. It's a nice touch, too, that at the climax John, when offered a 50/50 choice, chooses poorly, and enters the wrong building.

1X02 The Blind Banker
UK Airdate: 1 August 2010

Writer: Stephen Thompson
Director: Euros Lyn

Guest Cast: Gemma Chan (Soo Lin Yao); Al Weaver (Andy Galbraith); Bertie Carvel (Seb Wilkes); Dan Percival (Eddie Van Coon); Paul Chequer (Detective Inspector Dimmock); Howard Coggins (Brian Lukis); Janice Acquah (Museum Director); Jack Bence (Raz); John MacMillan (Community Police Officer); Olivia Poulet (Amanda); Jacqui Chan (Shopkeeper); Sarah Lam (Opera Singer); Gillian Elisa (Surgery Receptionist); Stefan Pejic (Box Office Manager); Philip Benjamin (German Tourist); Joanna Burnett (Tour Guide)*; Claire Cage (Eddie's Neighbour)*; Joe Hall (Homeless Guy)*

*Uncredited

Plot: John is having cash problems, and is forced to borrow his flatmate's debit card. With bills piling up, Sherlock suggests a trip to the bank. The bank in question is Shad Sanderson, at the heart of London's financial district – University pal Sebastian Wilkes needs Sherlock's help. The empty office of the bank's former chairman has been broken into, and a portrait of the man himself defaced with yellow spray paint. Additionally, the intruder has scrawled several indecipherable figures on the wall. Security records show that the door to that particular office did not open at all, so how were the bank's defences breached?

Sherlock realises that the graffiti was intended to be seen from the office of Eddie Van Coon, head of Shad

Sanderson's Hong Kong Desk. Sneaking into Van Coon's flat, they find the banker lying dead on his bed, an apparent suicide. Sherlock has no hesitation in informing Detective Inspector Dimmock that he's dealing with a murder, though, once again, there's no indication of how the culprit entered and left.

That night, freelance journalist Brian Lukis is murdered in his flat under very similar circumstances – shot by someone who can seemingly walk through walls. Sherlock is convinced it's the work of the same killer, and demands that Dimmock give him the opportunity to search Lukis' flat. Checking the skylight, Sherlock deduces that they are dealing with someone capable of scaling walls and entering premises via open windows. He finds a book from the West Kensington Library, taken out on the day of Lukis' death. At the library, he and John spot another cipher.

Behind the National Gallery, they seek advice from graffiti artist Raz, who promises to track down any more examples of the cipher.

Sherlock sends John to collect Lukis' effects from the police. As he leaves Baker Street, he's unaware that he is being photographed.

Sherlock questions Van Coon's PA, Amanda. His travel receipts suggest that he was taking an item to an address near Piccadilly Station. According to Lukis' diary, he too, went to the same store – the Lucky Cat Emporium – on the day he died. Van Coon and Lukis were both smugglers, delivering their goods to the Lucky Cat. One man evidently stole from his employers, and because it could not be determined which one it was, both were killed.

The address of the flat above the store belongs to Soo Lin Yao, but she has been absent for several days. Breaking in, Sherlock encounters another intruder, who attacks him before fleeing. Questioning one of her colleagues at the National Antiquities Museum, they find more ciphers, which Sherlock has now identified as Hang Zhou, an ancient writing system.

Raz has discovered more examples of the graffiti - the killer practised his craft on railway tunnel walls. The messages are numbers, and Sherlock is certain they are a message to underworld confederates from someone who wants their merchandise back.

Returning to the National Antiquities Museum, Sherlock deduces that Soo Lin Yao is still somewhere on the premises. Locating her hiding place, he and John learn that she is a former member of the Black Lotus Tong, who was contacted by the killer (who is also her brother), seeking her assistance in locating the missing item. Her brother's name is Liang, but he is known to the Tong general Shan as Zhi Zhu – the spider. Before she can give reveal the cipher key to the detectives, she is killed by Zhi Zhu.

Sherlock convinces Dimmock that Van Coon and Dimmock were also Tong members, smuggling ancient Chinese artefacts into the country to sell at auction. He and John spend all night studying the books belonging to the dead men in the hopes of cracking the code.

At Sherlock's suggestion, John takes his new girlfriend Sarah to the Yellow Dragon Circus. The detective tags along, convinced that one of the acrobats in the show, billed as the Deadly Chinese Bird Spider, might be Zhi Zhu. He's attacked while searching backstage, and the fight eventually disrupts the show.

At last, Sherlock realises that the book used to decode the cipher is the London A-Z. The full message is "Nine Mill (sic) for jade pin. Dragon den, black tramway." While he's out of the flat, John and Sarah are kidnapped by the Tong and taken to their hideout. They are confronted by the female General Shan, who is under the impression that John is Sherlock Holmes (he still has Sherlock's debit card). Shan threatens Sarah's life, demanding that John reveal the location of the jade pin. Sherlock arrives in the nick of time, and in the confusion, Shan escapes and John is able to rescue his girlfriend and kill Zhi Zhu.

Leaving Dimmock to tidy up the loose ends, Sherlock tracks down the jade pin – Eddie Van Coon gave it to his PA and former mistress as a gift, not realising its true worth.

In hiding, Shan reports to her London contact, a man known as M. To protect his anonymity, M has her killed by a sniper.

The best and the wisest man: Sherlock considers himself resourceful, dynamic and enigmatic (but evidently not modest). He uses John's laptop to check his e-mails when he can't be bothered walking to the bedroom to use his own computer. He doesn't eat when he's working: "digestion slows me down." He looks unusually pale in this episode. He knows a lot about escapology, describing the act at the Yellow Dragon Circus while John and Sarah watch. He's visibly annoyed by Sarah's presence at Baker Street, but surprisingly jovial when he tells Amanda she's had £9m pinned in her hair.

I am lost without my Boswell: John is forced to ask Sherlock for money, but it's a waste of time, since his associate isn't even listening. He's quick to take Sebastian Wilkes' retainer when Sherlock turns it down. He applies for work as a locum, welcoming the mundane routine (the very opposite of his attitude in the previous episode – did his hand tremor return?). After spending the night searching for the cipher code with Sherlock, he falls asleep at the surgery. Much to his chagrin, he winds up with an ASBO after being (falsely) charged with defacing a listed building – shades of Nigel Bruce. It's interesting to note that, after Van Coon's body is discovered, he handles the questioning of Sebastian Wilkes while Sherlock looks on. Clearly, the partnership has matured since *A Study in Pink*. He learned the clarinet at school.

The efficiency of our detective police force: Detective Inspector Dimmock is in charge in Lestrade's absence. He takes an instant dislike to Sherlock, firstly because it saves time, secondly because he resents an amateur handling evidence at a crime scene, and lastly because the consultant mistakes him for a mere sergeant (wouldn't a trained observer be able to figure something like that out?). He varies between helpfulness and disdain, depending upon how the investigation is proceeding. Sherlock says he has high hopes for Dimmock. "I go where you point me," the Inspector admits. There's no shortage of policemen in the original stories, so why couldn't Dimmock have been given a Canonical name? I'd nominate Inspector Forbes of *The Naval Treaty*, with whom Dimmock shares a number of traits.

There is a strong family resemblance about misdeeds: After the plethora of references in the previous episode, and many more to come in *The Great Game*, this is story is extraordinarily light on Canonical influences. The killer's entry and exit via a skylight recalls the death of Bartholomew Sholto, killed by the nimble pygmy Tonga in the novel *The Sign of Four*. The notion of a code in the form of apparently meaningless graffiti is derived from *The Dancing Men*, and the discovery that the key to deciphering the code is to be found in an easily-obtainable book mirrors the opening scene of the final Holmes novel *The Valley of Fear*.

I have never loved: John is quick to explain to Sebastian

Wilkes that he is Sherlock's colleague, heading off any of the misunderstandings that filled the previous week's episode.

When Sherlock asks him how his job interview went, John absent-mindedly replies "she was great," referring to Dr Sarah Sawyer. He doesn't waste a whole lot of time in asking her out on a date, though given that it ends up with her tied to a chair with a crossbow pointed at her head, it's remarkable that she agrees to see him again. Sherlock flatters Molly in order to get a look at the corpses of Lukis and Van Coon.

A certain unexpected vein of pawky humour: Watson has a disagreement with a chip and pin machine at Asda, while back at Baker Street, Holmes engages in a battle with the swordsman from *Raiders of the Lost Ark*. The fight relates to an unseen case, the Jaria diamond.

Sherlock asks John to pass him a pen, not noticing that his flatmate has gone to apply for a job. He's quite content a wait an hour until John gets back, though.

When Sherlock says he needs advice in order to crack the cipher, John asks him to repeat the remark. "You heard me perfectly, I'm not saying it again."

Sherlock and Raz flee at the sight of the National Gallery's security officers, leaving John literally carrying the can. John insists that Raz appear at his hearing and clear his name, but it's an unlikely eventuality.

Sherlock tells John they should go out an get some fresh air. John explains that he has a date: "Where two people who like each other go out and have fun?" Sherlock: "That's what *I* was suggesting!" Sherlock crashes their date, of course, causing John much annoyance. "You're going to chase some killer while I'm trying to get off with Sarah!" he protests somewhat loudly, just as she appears at his side.

Sherlock doesn't admit to John that he was nearly strangled by Zhi Zhu in Soo Lin Yao's flat. "You've gone all croaky. Are you getting a cold?"

My head is in a whirl: Why does Sherlock take Eddie Van Coon's nameplate when checking the Shad Sanderson offices? Is he incapable of remembering it?

John addresses his friend by name in the Lucky Cat Emporium, and yet they still think *he's* Sherlock Holmes?

Soo Lin Yao says that the Tong are never very far away "in a small community like ours" but is that any excuse for choosing a flat immediately above a shop used by the Tong as a base for receiving smuggled goods?

Zhi Zhu lets Sherlock live, even though he's so close to asphyxiating him in his sister's flat. If the Tong think John is Sherlock, why spare him?

"What kind of message would everyone try to avoid?" Though thoroughly competent in all departments, it's impossible not to feel a tinge of disappointment at this episode, coming just a week after something as truly remarkable as *A Study in Pink*. The direction boasts none of the imaginative flair seen in that first episode (to be fair, many of the visuals were the invention of director Paul McGuigan, who did not work on this episode). There simply isn't enough to distinguish this plot from most other British crime dramas – it could just as easily serve as an episode of *Lewis*, *Taggart*, or even, at a stretch, *Midsomer Murders* ("A Chinese circus comes to Midsomer..."). The meaning of the episode title is vague and not strictly accurate – it refers to the defacing of the portrait of the bank's chairman, a line of spray paint covering his eyes. *The Blind Banker* is the least satisfying of *Sherlock*'s first season, but even that couldn't stop the show's phenomenal popularity. As *The Reichenbach Fall* will prove, it would be a serious mistake to identify Steve Thompson as the weak link as the writing trio.

1X03 The Great Game
UK Airdate: 8 August 2010

Writer: Mark Gatiss
Director: Paul McGuigan

Guest Cast: John Lebar (Golem); Matthew Needham (Bezza); Kemal Sylvester (Tube Guard); San Shella (Andrew West); Deborah Moore (Crying Woman); Lauren Crace (Lucy); Nicholas Gadd (Scared Man); Caroline Trowbridge (Mrs Monkford); Paul Albertson (Mr Ewart); Rita Davies (Blind Lady); Di Botcher (Connie Prince); John Sessions (Kenny Prince); Stefano Braschi (Raoul); Jeany Spark (Homeless Girl); Alison Lintott (Julie); Haydn Gwynne (Miss Wenceslas); Doug Allen (Joe); Lynn Fairleigh (Professor Cairns); Peter Davison (Planetarium Voiceover)*

*Uncredited

Plot: After John walks out of Baker Street following a minor row with Sherlock over the presence of a severed head in the fridge, the building is rocked by an explosion, the result of a gas leak in the house opposite, it is supposed. Rushing back home after seeing the story on the news, John finds Sherlock unharmed and in conversation with his brother Mycroft regarding the death of MOD employee Andrew West, who has been found dead on the tracks at Battersea Station. West was in possession of a memory stick containing the plans for the Bruce-Partington missile program, but it was not found on the body, and it is feared that the young man may have been a traitor. Holmes turns the case down, even though he's far from busy.

After Mycroft departs, Sherlock and John are summoned to New Scotland Yard by Lestrade. He informs them that the gas leak was faked, and that the only item to survive the explosion was a strongbox containing a pink phone identical to the one that featured in Sherlock's first case with John. Someone has recorded a message on the phone – five pips, and a photo of the basement flat at Mrs Hudson's house. Inside 221C Baker Street, they find a pair of training shoes, and as Sherlock is about to examine them, he receives a call on the pink phone – a frightened woman is reading out a typed message: "Twelve hours to solve my puzzle, Sherlock, or I'm going to be so naughty." The woman has a bomb strapped to her body, and a sniper's weapon is trained upon her. At the end of twelve hours, if Sherlock is unsuccessful, the sniper will fire and the bomb will detonate.

Sherlock is studying the shoes in the lab at Bart's as Molly introduces him to her new boyfriend, Jim from IT, whom Sherlock has no hesitation in identifying as gay, breaking Molly's heart yet again.

The shoes belonged to Carl Powers, who, in 1989 drowned in a London swimming pool, having come up from Brighton for a school sports tournament. Sherlock remembers the case, and was always puzzled by the absence of the boy's shoes. He realises that a poison was introduced into Carl's eczema cream. The killer is, John suggests, also the bomber. Following the discovery of the solution, the hostage is released, and her location disclosed to the police.

Sherlock receives another call from another hostage, also rigged with a bomb. He has eight hours to solve another puzzle – the abandoned car of banker Ian Monkford has been discovered, soaked in his blood. Sherlock and John speak to Ewart, owner of Janus Cars, the firm from which Monkford hired the vehicle. Holmes finds that the blood – exactly a pint – was donated by Ian Monkford some time earlier, and then frozen. Janus Cars is a company specializing in faking the deaths of individuals who wish to disappear. With the arrest of Ewart, the second hostage is freed.

The next hostage is an elderly blind woman. Relating Moriarty's words, she gives him 12 hours to unravel the riddle of the death of TV's makeover queen, Connie Prince, who supposedly contracted tetanus from a cut on her hand which, Sherlock notes, was made after her death. John poses as a journalist in order to question Connie's brother Kenny, and begins to form a theory – the tetanus was on the claws of Connie's pet cat. But Sherlock declares it too random and too clever for Kenny. Raoul de Santos, Kenny's houseboy is the killer. He poisoned Connie via her botox injections, using the same toxin that killed Carl Powers. The case is solved, but the old woman being held hostage makes the mistake of attempting to tell Sherlock about Moriarty, and the bomb is set off by the sniper.

Another call, another case, but no mention of a hostage this time. A body has washed up on the South Bank. Sherlock identifies the dead man as a security guard, and a victim of assassin Oskar Dzundza, AKA the Golem. Alex Woodbridge, gallery attendant at the Hickman Gallery, has been reported missing, just before the unveiling of a recently discovered Vermeer worth £30m. John investigates Woodbridge, and finds that the dead man has an interest in astronomy and had received a message from a Professor Cairns. Sherlock and John track Cairns down at a planetarium, but are too late to prevent the Golem disposing of her. As the deadline approaches, the hostage, a child, calls – Sherlock has only 10 seconds to prove that the painting is a forgery. At the last second, he discovers that the painting includes the Van Buren supernova, which occurred almost 200 years after Vermeer supposedly painted the missing masterpiece. The Hickman Gallery's curator, Ms Wenceslas, confesses to her part in the crime, acting under Moriarty's guidance.

Mycroft continues to pester Sherlock about the death of Andrew West. John is put onto the case, and questions his fiancée, Liz, who says that on the night of his death, West saw something from his window that disturbed him. Shortly thereafter, he left the house. John is puzzled by the fact that there's no blood on the train tracks. Sherlock has already solved the case, however – he's been investigating all along, despite his insistence that he's not interested. Searching the flat of Liz's brother Joe Harrison, they find traces of blood. Joe admits to stealing the memory stick from his prospective brother-in-law. Joe killed West by accident after the civil servant confronted him and they struggled. He subsequently dumped West's body onto the roof of a train that had halted under the window of his flat. The body came off the roof where the line curves.

As John goes out to visit Sarah that evening, Sherlock contacts Moriarty. A meeting is arranged at the swimming pool where Carl Powers died. But Sherlock is stunned when he is confronted by John Watson! John, however, isn't Moriarty – he's the next hostage, a bomb concealed under his clothing, and a sniper's rifle trained on him. Moriarty finally appears – it's Molly's boyfriend, Jim from IT. He's been throwing problems in Sherlock's way, just to get him to "come out and play." In return for John's life, Sherlock offers him the missile plans, which the disinterested Moriarty tosses into the pool. He tells Sherlock that he will burn the heart right out of him if he continues to pry. Jim leaves, and Sherlock frees John from the explosives. They don't get to enjoy the moment, however – Moriarty returns and informs Sherlock that he can't be allowed to live, as they are suddenly targeted by multiple snipers. With John's nod of approval, Sherlock aims his gun at the explosives positioned between them and Moriarty.

The best and the wisest man: The episode begins with a short scene in a Minsk prison (loosely derived from one of Gatiss' League of Gentlemen stage sketches) in which Sherlock continually corrects the grammar of a condemned man. He's taken a severed head from Bart's morgue in order to measure the coagulation of saliva after death. He has no interest in any of the hostages. "There's hospitals full of people dying, Doctor, why don't you go and cry by their bedside and see what good it does them?" he asks, in a spectacular display of heartlessness, to which the destruction of Molly's love life is merely the *coup de grace*. He considers the Carl Powers case his entry into the world of detection (at which point he would've been in his early teens). He thought there was something fishy about the boy's death when he read about it in the newspapers at the time. The Home Secretary owes him a favour. He becomes a fan of reality TV.

I am lost without my Boswell: He's written up their first adventure together on his blog as *A Study in Pink*. Sherlock hates it. Frustrated by the countdown, he desperately needs to do something, which is probably one reason why Sherlock puts him onto the Bruce-Partington affair. He knows about Moriarty. He and Mrs Hudson watch far too much daytime TV, including Connie Prince's makeover show.

The efficiency of our detective police force: Lestrade and his colleagues all read Watson's blog. He's on hand for most of this adventure, but we don't really find out much about him this time.

Sergeant Sally Donovan appears briefly. Her opinion of Sherlock hasn't improved at all. She recommends John get a hobby instead of hanging around with the detective – stamp collecting, perhaps, or fishing.

There is a strong family resemblance about misdeeds: Where to begin? Well, this episode finally sees Moriarty make his big appearance. Though constantly popping up in pastiches, Professor James Moriarty barely appears within the canon – his only big scene, in *The Final Problem*, is related to Watson by Holmes (the basis for the notion in both Nicholas Meyer's novel *The Seven-Per-Cent Solution* and Jeremy Paul's stage play *The Secret of Sherlock Holmes* that the Napoleon of Crime never actually existed – see *The Great Game*). The Professor is also said to have played a part in the murder investigated by Holmes in the novel *The Valley of Fear*. Jim's line, "Everything I have to say has already crossed your mind," comes from *The Final Problem*. The depiction of a manic, impulsive Moriarty in this series is markedly different from that of a man so cold-blooded Conan Doyle likens him to a reptile. If anything, non-Professor Jim Moriarty owes as much to Heath Ledger's Joker in *The Dark Knight* as he does to the Canonical character, and your enjoyment of this version depends upon your tolerance for the excesses the portrayal of such a theatrical villain demands. Radically different interpretations of Sherlock Holmes' arch nemesis are the order of the day in both series discussed in this volume.

To clarify the "Dear Jim, please can you fix it..." line for non-UK readers, this relates to the long-running TV programme *Jim'll Fix It*, in which young viewers had their wishes granted by host and popular DJ Jimmy Savile. After Savile's death in 2011, allegations were made of sexual offences on a colossal scale. Had this episode been produced after the truth became known, it is more than likely that Gatiss would have omitted this reference from the dialogue.

Moffat and Gatiss are both fans of the Basil Rathbone/Nigel Bruce movies, and the main body of the plot bears more than a passing resemblance to Rathbone's 1939 picture (his final one for 20th Century Fox), *The Adventures of Sherlock Holmes*, in which Professor Moriarty (George Zucco) distracts Holmes with a puzzle involving numerous bizarre elements to enable him to pull off a spectacular crime without interference. Although, in this episode, Moriarty isn't really all that interested in obtaining the memory stick, which he insists he could've acquired by other means.

Speaking of the Rathbone series, the killer known as the Golem is not dissimilar in size and brutality to the Creeper (played by Rondo Hatton) in the 1944 film *The Pearl of Death*, an updating of Conan Doyle's tale *The Six Napoleons*.

The subplot of *The Great Game* is based very closely on *The Bruce-Partington Plans*, in which the murdered man, Cadogan West is believed to have stolen the plans of an experimental submarine. Gatiss works another stolen plans story, *The Naval Treaty*, into the solution. In that story, as in this, the thief is named Joseph Harrison, brother of the woman to whom the victim is affianced.

The five pips on the telephone refer to Conan Doyle's *The Five Orange Pips*. As Sherlock says here, these seeds were sent by secret societies (the KKK in the original story) along with threatening messages to their intended victims. The decreasing number of pips signifying the number of crimes remaining to be perpetrated is an element of the Rathbone film *The House of Fear*, in which they are, of course, actual seed pips.

The shoe deduction scene is top-heavy with references. For starters, it resembles the famous hat sequence from

The Blue Carbuncle. Holmes' remark, "You missed almost everything of importance, but, you know..." is a variation on a line from *The Hound of the Baskervilles*, as is, "You know what I do – off you go," a modernisation of the famous phrase, "You know my methods – apply them." When he tells John, "You're on sparkling form," he's channelling the Holmes of *The Valley of Fear*, who informed his comrade, "you're scintillating this morning."

In *The Musgrave Ritual*, Watson describes Holmes' less-than delightful qualities as a fellow lodger: "I have always held, too, that pistol practice should be distinctly an open-air pastime; and when Holmes, in one of his queer humours, would sit in an armchair with his hair-trigger and a hundred Boxer cartridges and proceed to adorn the opposite wall with a patriotic VR done in bullet-pocks, I felt strongly that neither the atmosphere nor the appearance of our room was improved by it." Following his return from Minsk, Sherlock shoots a smiley face into the wall. Coincidentally, Robert Downey Jr's Holmes creates a VR of bullet-holes (no doubt his tribute to *Pulp Fiction* actor Ving Rhames) in his first movie.

Sherlock identifies the envelope containing the phone as originating in Bohemia, as did the letter received by Holmes in – surprise, surprise – *A Scandal in Bohemia*. The script's numerous references to the Czech Republic are revealed to be a red herring, or they would have if that line hadn't been cut. The famous phrase "You see, but you do not observe", repeated by Sherlock in this episode can also be found in *A Scandal in Bohemia*, along with "I am lost without my Boswell" (updated to "I'd be lost without my blogger") and the exchange between Holmes and Watson in which the detective notes that his friend has gained seven and a half pounds since getting married, while the doctor insists it is only seven. In *The Great Game*, that conversation is between Sherlock and Molly, and the weight increase a less insulting three pounds.

Sherlock's lack of knowledge about the solar system is described in *A Study in Scarlet*. In the novel, he likens his mind to an attic rather than a hard drive, though the same speech, taken from the same source, appears in the second episode of *Elementary*, where the attic analogy is retained.

The number seven is an important one to the Holmes of the Canon – he's devised seven separate explanations to explain the conundrum of *The Copper Beeches*, and in *The Missing Three-Quarter*, he has seven different schemes for getting a look at an important telegram. At the scene of Alex Woodbridge's murder, he says he has formulated seven ideas so far, and has another seven in *The Hounds of Baskerville*.

Holmes' unfavourable reaction to Watson's published account of their first adventure in *The Sign of Four* matches Sherlock's complaints about John's blog entry, *A Study in Pink*.

The Homeless Network are Sherlock's modern day equivalent of the Baker Street Irregulars, AKA the Baker Street Division of the Detective Police Force. "These youngsters... go everywhere and hear everything," he tells Watson in *A Study in Scarlet*. The Irregulars also appear in *The Sign of Four* and *The Crooked Man*. The Homeless Network are mentioned again in *A Scandal in Belgravia* and *The Reichenbach Fall*.

The Three Garridebs occurs, Watson says, "in the same month that Holmes refused a knighthood for services which may perhaps some day be described." Following the recovery of the memory stick, Sherlock says he has been "threatened with a knighthood – again," although he hasn't actually returned the memory stick at this point, so he may only have been threatened the once. In *A Scandal in Belgravia*, he jokes about his knighthood being "in the bag" now that certain incriminating photos of a royal personage have been recovered.

Sherlock is seen to play the violin in this episode, pretty badly. In fact, the Canonical Holmes is a reasonably proficient player, but filmmakers seem to find it more fun to have him play abominably. He's improved by the time of *A Scandal in Belgravia*, so he was probably deliberately making a din here. In *The Reichenbach Fall*, Moriarty considers Sherlock's interpretation of Bach appalling.

Having scripted several episodes of the *Doctor Who* revival and a number of novels featuring the Time Lord, it seems only natural that Gatiss should slip several oblique references to the series into this episode. Sherlock describes the Golem as "One of the deadliest assassins in the world," a vague nod toward the 1976 Tom Baker story *The Deadly Assassin*, both scripts apparently suggesting that there are other sorts of assassins, apart from deadly ones (I suppose there might be harmless assassins, but I can't see them getting a lot of work). The Fifth Doctor himself Peter Davison (alongside whom Gatiss has appeared on several occasions, notably in two *Doctor Who* audio stories produced by Big Finish and an episode of the hilarious sci-fi radio comedy *Nebulous*) supplies the recorded commentary in the planetarium, during John and Sherlock's tussle with the Golem. And might the Hickman Galley be named after former *Doctor Who Magazine* editor Clayton Hickman?

I have never loved: John sleeps on the sofa at Sarah's place – their relationship is still in its early stages, and the next time we see John, in *A Scandal in Belgravia*, it's over.

Sherlock considers breaking the news about Jim's sexuality to Molly "kinder" in the long run. John disagrees.

Once Jim comes out as Moriarty, he mentions in passing that he was merely pretending to be gay.

John jokes about what people might say if they saw Sherlock ripping his clothes off in the public baths.

A seven-per-cent solution: Sherlock asks Ewart if he has change for the cigarette machine. In fact, he only wants to see the Columbian money inside the man's wallet. He reminds John that he's "doing well" on nicotine patches

A certain unexpected vein of pawky humour: Watson discovers a head in the fridge. Not a head of lettuce, an actual head.

In the lab, Sherlock asks John to retrieve his phone from his jacket – the jacket he happens to be wearing at the time.

Sherlock explains to Lestrade why the caller is leading them to the solutions of so many crimes: "Good Samaritan." When the Inspector points out that Moriarty is press-ganging suicide bombers: "Bad Samaritan."

Kenny Prince praises his sister's makeover skills, particularly when it comes to girls who look like "the back end of routemasters."

The "Meretricious" - "And a happy new year" exchange originates in Stephen Fry's pastiche *The Adventure of the Laughing Jarvey.*

John, on Sherlock's arrangement with the Homeless Network: "So you scratch their back, and..?" Holmes: "Then disinfect myself."

My head is in a whirl: How far did John get after leaving 221B? He really didn't hear the explosion? He should probably get that looked into.

Sherlock says there's no suspect for the murder of Carl Powers among his friends, but he's only had an afternoon in which to ascertain this. Given that Jim Moriarty did indeed kill Carl, it would seem that Sherlock's best chance of tracking him down – in the unlikely event that he and John survive the confrontation at the swimming pool – would be to investigate this incident in depth, with an eye to locating a teenager with an Irish accent and access to Clostridium botulinum in 1989. Granted, Brighton was full of them in those days, but it's a starting point. Yes, the second season will almost certainly focus upon this dangling plot-thread, I'll stake my reputation as a writer of episode guides on it.

"Don't make people into heroes, John. Heroes don't exist, and if they did, I wouldn't be one of them." The equivalent of holding your breath for ninety minutes, there is not an ounce of flab on Gatiss' pacey script, which never fails to compel - probably just as well given that, like the Rathbone film from which it draws much of its inspiration, it doesn't make an awful lot of sense on close inspection. On the strength of two superior episodes, Sherlock has deservedly become a massive hit. Small wonder, then, that the BBC began advertising Season Two long before shooting had even begun.

Unaired Pilot: A Study in Pink
UK Airdate: N/A

Writer: Steven Moffat
Director: Coky Giedroyc

Guest Cast: Zawe Ashton (Sgt Sally Donovan); Joseph Long (Angelo); David Nellist (Mike Stamford); James Harper (Cabbie); Philip Davis (The Taxi Driver)

Plot: The episode, for the most part, follows the same path as the broadcast version, with only minor differences – John and Mike Stamford are reunited in the heart of London, rather than in Russell Square, and the subject of Sherlock Holmes' search for a fellow-lodger comes up as they enjoy lunch in the actual Criterion Bar. Sherlock and John first meet in a media suite rather than in the lab at Bart's. Speedy's is named Mrs Hudson's Snax 'n' Sarnies (in the series proper, she has no connection with the establishment, other than a desire to win the affections of the proprietor, Mr Chatterjee – see *The Hounds of Baskerville*). Their landlady doesn't remove Sherlock's skull (wow, that sounds odd). Jennifer Wilson, the lady in pink, is unnamed in this episode, her killer having removed all identification from the body. There's no mention of Moriarty and no scenes with Mycroft. Angelo is played by Joseph Long, better known for playing another Italian restaurateur, Luigi, in the cult cop show *Ashes to Ashes*.

The major plot deviation occurs during the stakeout at Angelo's restaurant – Sherlock has already deduced that the killer is a cabbie, and when a taxi pulls up in Northumberland Street and turns down a fare, he poses as a drunk in order to approach the driver (whose name is never given, but we'll stick with Jeff). Sherlock calls Jeff on the pink phone and accosts the killer as he answers, not realising that he's just been injected with something to knock him out. Jeff puts Sherlock into the back of his cab and drives him back to Baker Street. John takes chase on foot, leaving his stick behind.

Sherlock comes to in his flat as Jeff presents him with the pills. He has to fight through the haze of the injection in order to engage in mental combat with Jeff. The police show up, but not in time to prevent Sherlock picking a pill and preparing to take it. John saves the day by shooting Jeff from the window of the empty house opposite.

The best and the wisest man: Sherlock has already decided that the deaths are not suicides but the work of a serial killer before he's had the chance to examine the body – hardly surprising, given that the cabbie has taken his victims' IDs each time. He joins John in wearing a forensic onesie when examining the body. He doesn't correct Sally's description of him as a psychopath. In fact, he praises her assessment. He considers little old ladies better than any security cameras. One of his earlier cases involved a headless nun. Unlike his 90 minute counterpart, he doesn't always favour a monochromatic ensemble, sporting a green shirt. Benedict Cumberbatch's hair is noticeably lighter in the pilot.

I am lost without my Boswell: John doesn't get the opportunity to show what he's made of by standing up to Mycroft, which is a shame. He's noticeably agitated as he heads back to Baker Street, irritated when a cabbie (not Jeff) tells him he looks "wired." He throws his gun into the Thames after shooting Jeff.

The efficiency of our detective police force: Lestrade's approach is slightly different in this version – he's the one who decides to contact the consulting detective, before the murder of Jennifer Wilson occurs, instead of having Sherlock pester him during a press conference.

Sergeant Sally Donovan is played by Zawe Ashton in this episode only. She's a uniformed officer, but though her appearance is different, her opinion of Sherlock isn't.

Anderson is bearded and wears glasses. He urges Lestrade not to bring Sherlock in on the case.

Sherlock's in-box contains e-mails from Gregson, Smith and Jones (presumably not Mel and Griff Rhys). There's no policeman named Smith in the Canon, but Tobias Gregson appears in *A Study in Scarlet*, *The Greek Interpreter* and *The Red Circle*. Played by Aidan Quinn, Toby/Tommy Gregson is a regular character in *Elementary*. Jones could be either Athelney Jones of *The Sign of Four* or Peter Jones of *The Red-Headed League*. Sally is heard mentioning a Jones to another officer, but there's absolutely no reason to suppose that she's referring to Sherlock's correspondent – it's just possible, I suppose, that there are more than two Joneses on the force.

Sherlock's reply to Gregson's message reads: "If you can see the church bell from the bedroom window, Davies is your man." Not famed Sherlockian pastiche writer and author of *The Veiled Detective* David Stuart Davies, surely?

There is a strong family resemblance about misdeeds: As in the original novel, John declares Sherlock's article on the science of deduction: "Amusing." Mycroft doesn't appear in this episode, though his name is seen on an e-mail Sherlock sends while at Bart's (his brother's address is, appropriately, mycroft@deux.org). The message reads: "When you have eliminated the impossible whatever remains must be the truth." Holmes' famous mantra first appears in *The Sign of Four*, and it is in full: "When you have eliminated the impossible, whatever remains, however improbable, must be the truth." He finally says it in the series proper during *The Hounds of Baskerville*. Holmes repeats the phrase throughout the Canon in *The Beryl Coronet*, *The Blanched Soldier* and *The Bruce-Partington Plans*.

Holmes' claim in *The Mazarin Stone*, "I am a brain, Watson; the rest of me is a mere appendix," resurfaces here, as Sherlock's "The brain's what counts, everything else is transport."

The similarity between the climax of *A Study in Pink* and that of *The Empty House* is more clear-cut in this pilot episode. In Conan Doyle's story, Moriarty's right-hand man Sebastian Moran attempts to shoot Holmes from the window of the empty house opposite number 221B. While positioning John in that same spot is more familiar, it makes less sense (see **My head is in a whirl**).

The script appears to feature another *Doctor Who* reference from another *Doctor Who* writer. Sherlock's line "Only a fool argues with his doctor" also shows up in the 1998 Sylvester McCoy story *Remembrance of the Daleks* by *Ben Aaronovitch*.

I have never loved: Sherlock is, as usual, utterly oblivious to Molly's attempts to arrange a date.

During the scene at Angelo's Sherlock indicates that he is entirely asexual, which would come as a bitter disappointment to Molly and Irene both.

A seven-per-cent solution: "Do a lot of drugs, Sherlock Holmes?" asks Jeff. Sherlock: "Not in a while." Jeff: "I ask 'cause you're very resilient." At this point, Sherlock hasn't noticed there's a syringe in his arm. You'd think the little prick might have tipped him off.

A certain unexpected vein of pawky humour: John asks Sherlock if he's going to eat at Angelo's. "What day is it?" he asks. "It's Wednesday." "I'm OK for a bit."
John, discussing matters of sexual orientation: "It's all fine, whatever shakes your... boat. I'm going to shut up now." Sherlock: "I think that's for the best."

My head is in a whirl: The scene with Sherlock and John discussing the mobile phone deductions in a taxi is fairly obviously shot in a studio.
When Sherlock approaches Jeff's cab, he taps on the driver's window. Moments later, Jeff reaches out and points at the unlit sign, the window having magically rolled down in an instant.
At Baker Street, Jeff is sat immediately in front of Sherlock. Why, then, when he's shot by John, does the bullet pass through the cabbie and enter the wall instead of Sherlock?
Just why does John go into the empty house to shoot at Jeff instead of sneaking into 221? How does he even know it's empty?

"You can't beat a really imaginative serial killer when there's nothing on the telly." Apart from the issue of story length, the differences between the pilot and what eventually appeared onscreen are relatively minor. The episode doesn't begin with an Afghanistan flashback, but it looks as though one might have been inserted had it actually been broadcast. There's a different and far briefer title sequence, the familiar theme music less bold, and missing the influences of the movie soundtrack. It's hard to say, on this evidence, just how different a one-hour series might have been, although the climax of *The Great Game* would've proved harder to arrange, given that there's no gun for our hero to aim at the explosives.

Season Two

2X01: A Scandal in Belgravia
UK Airdate: 1 January 2012

Writer: Steven Moffat
Director: Paul McGuigan

Guest Cast: Lara Pulver (Irene Adler); Danny Webb (DI Carter); Andrew Havill (The Equerry); Todd Boyce (Neilson); Oona Chaplin (Jeanette); Richard Cunningham (Timid Man); Rosemary Smith (Married Woman); Simon Thorp (Businessman); Anthony Cozens (Geeky Young Man); Munir Khairdin (Creepy Guy); Nathan Harmer (Phil); Luke Newberry (Young Policeman); Darrell Las Quevas (Plummer); Rosalind Halstead (Kate); Peter Pedrero (Archer); Honor Kneafsey (Little Girl); Ilana Kneafsey (Little Girl); Thomasin Rand (Beautiful Woman); Greg Bennett (CIA Driver)*; Simon Blood DeVay (Detective – CID)* Amber Elizabeth (Commuter)*

*Uncredited

Plot: The tension of the standoff is ruined by the ringing of Moriarty's phone. He's had an offer which, apparently, requires Sherlock and John to remain alive a while longer.

The following months prove very fruitful with many demands upon Sherlock's time, including a man who insists his dead aunt's ashes have been switched, two children who weren't permitted to see their grandfather after his death and, most perplexing of all, the presence in Southwark of a man who supposedly boarded a flight that crashed in Düsseldorf, the result of a terrorist bomb.

A man visits Baker Street, fearing that he's wanted for

murder. 14 hours earlier, he was attempting to repair his car in the countryside as a nearby rambler suddenly and unaccountably died from a single blow to the back of the head from a blunt instrument which has somehow vanished. John goes to the scene on Sherlock's behalf. The mystery isn't very complex: the hiker was killed by a stray boomerang, but Sherlock doesn't get to reveal the solution before he and John are summoned to Buckingham Palace, where they are met by Mycroft.

Professional dominatrix Irene Adler is in possession of a considerable number of compromising photographs featuring a female royal. Sherlock is tasked with recovering them.

He shows up at Irene's door posing as the victim of a mugging. John is in tow, acting the good Samaritan. But their arrival has been anticipated, and Irene is prepared for them, undressed to kill. The plan nevertheless goes ahead, with John setting off the fire alarm to get Irene to give up the one thing she has left to reveal: the location of her safe. But some unexpected guests arrive in the form of a group of gun-wielding CIA agents, whose leader, Neilson, demands that Sherlock open hand over the safe's contents to them. He deduces the combination (it's Irene's vital statistics), overcomes the intruders and recovers the phone on which the photos are stored. The phone is password protected, however - the screen reads "I am ---- Locked" - and Irene refuses to tell him the four-digit code. While John is checking the exits, Irene drugs Sherlock and takes back her phone. When reporting to Mycroft, Sherlock hears his brother discussing "Bond Air" with a colleague.

On Christmas Day, Irene has her phone delivered to Baker Street. Sherlock tells his brother that he's certain Irene will turn up dead, and, sure enough, her body is in the morgue, the face mutilated.

A week later, John is summoned to Battersea Power

Station by a very much alive Irene – she's made a mistake, she says, and wants her phone back. Sherlock has followed John, and when he gets back to Baker Street, he finds that Neilson, the CIA goon who threatened him at Irene's house is holding Mrs Hudson at gunpoint. He overcomes the agent, and hands him over to Lestrade – after dropping him out of the window several times.

Irene shows up at Baker Street, on the run. She explains that she photographed an e-mail sent to one of her clients, an MOD official. The e-mail concerns a 747 leaving Heathrow for Baltimore from 6.30 – flight no. 007, Mycroft's "Bond Air." The British and American governments have discovered that terrorists are planning bomb a commercial airliner, and have decided to use the incident to their advantage, filling the seats with the recently deceased, and piloting the 747 by remote-control. Many of the cases Sherlock turned down or failed to solve in recent months - the phoney ashes, the deceased grandparent, the body in Southwark - are related to this incident and a similar operation in Germany.

Unbeknownst to both Sherlock and John, Irene notifies Moriarty, who in turn contacts Mycroft, ruining the operation. Sherlock's eagerness to show off in front of The Woman has spoiled everything.

Irene tells Mycroft that she is in possession of many more secrets. She demands an extortionate sum in return for her phone and password. She claims never to have cared for Sherlock, but he has taken her pulse, and knows from its rate that she really does love him. He realises at last that the code for her phone is "I am **SHER** Locked." Her secrets revealed, Irene is handed over to Mycroft.

Months later, John meets Mycroft at Speedy's, and learns that Irene was recently beheaded by a terrorist cell in Karachi. Mycroft wishes Sherlock to believe that The Woman is alive and in the US Witness Protection

Program. Little do either of them realise that Irene escaped her execution with Sherlock's assistance.

The best and the wisest man: Sherlock's new-found fame means that he has the opportunity to be ruder than before to an even wider range of clients. He's left a bag of thumbs in the fridge. He's quite prepared to walk out of Buckingham Palace naked (although it's a safe bet that Prince Harry has already beaten him to it). He plays *God Save the Queen* and *We Wish You a Merry Christmas* on the violin, and composes a melody of his own after Irene's "death." He indexes his socks. He's appeared on *Crimewatch*. Though his apparent heartlessness is frequently harped upon, his anger at Neilson's treatment of Mrs Hudson finds an outlet. As a child, Mycroft says, Sherlock wanted to be a pirate. After the Adler case, he solves a triple murder in Leeds. He's younger than Mycroft (by seven years in the Canon).

I am lost without my Boswell: John is flexing his writing muscles, and raising his colleague's public profile at the same time. He's recently returned from Dublin when he and Sherlock become embroiled in the Adler affair. He's visibly smug upon learning that the Queen enjoys his blog. Through a series of onscreen deductions, we learn a lot about John: he uses an electric razor, has been wearing the same shirt for two days, has purchased a new toothbrush, has had a heavy night out on the town with Mike Stamford, and needs to phone his sister (evidently, relations between the relations have improved since *A Study in Pink*).

The efficiency of our detective police force: Lestrade actually seems to enjoy Sherlock's fame. Is he proud of the lad, or does he just like to watch him squirm? Since he films a drugged and rambling Sherlock on his phone, it's probably more the latter than the former. He advises DI Carter not to punch Sherlock. He's back with his wife, and planning a holiday in Dorset, not realising that she's sleeping with a PE teacher. He takes the news surprisingly well.

There is a strong family resemblance about misdeeds:
Of course, this episode's main source of inspiration is the first Sherlock Holmes short story, *A Scandal in Bohemia*, the only one to feature the character of Irene Adler, the adversary always referred to by Holmes as The Woman, though not in any of the three other stories in which she is mentioned. Changing *Bohemia* to *Belgravia* in the title is an irresistible choice, but author Kim Newman got there first in his short story *A Shambles in Belgravia*.

In the original tale, Holmes and Watson are employed by the King of Bohemia to recover from Miss Adler a compromising photograph which could prevent his forthcoming marriage. Holmes disguises himself as a priest and pretends to have been injured breaking up a fight between two ruffians (the entire incident is, of course, staged). Holmes is carried into Irene's house to recuperate, and the two meet face-to-face for the only time, with Holmes in disguise and Watson not present to relate what's said. The doctor is waiting outside, and starts an alarm of fire, causing Irene to give away the location of the photo. Holmes and Watson withdraw to Baker Street, intending to return to Irene's home the following day. They are passed on the street by a young man who bids them a good evening. When, in the company of their client, they attempt to collect the photograph the next morning, they discover that Irene has fled, taking the picture with her as security. Donning her own disguise, she was the young man who passed them outside 221B the night before.

Pastiche writers and filmmakers have frequently reunited Holmes and Irene, usually suggesting a romantic relationship between the two (though it's hard to imagine where they had the opportunity to fit it in, if you'll pardon the expression). In his famous biography, W S Baring Gould suggested that Holmes and Irene were involved sexually and that the child resulting from that union grew up to be Rex Stout's famously rotund detective Nero Wolfe. In the 1976 TV movie *Sherlock Holmes in New York*, screenwriter Alvin Sapinsley also supposed that Holmes and Irene (played by Roger Moore and Charlotte Rampling) had a torrid affair, a fact exploited by Professor Moriarty (John Huston) who kidnaps their son in order to dissuade Holmes from interfering in this week's crime of the century. Author Carole Nelson Douglas has written an entire series of Irene Adler novels.

The 2012 Irene is a professional dominatrix, who is known as The Woman for business purposes. It's impossible not to be reminded of the hit US crime show *CSI*, in which, during the first seven or so seasons, lead investigator Gil Grissom was involved in a will-they-won't-they or have-they-already-when-we-weren't-watching relationship with a dominatrix named Lady Heather.

As in the short story, Sherlock takes on the role of a cleric when trying to inveigle his way into Irene's residence. His justification for having John start a small blaze - "on hearing a smoke alarm, a mother would look towards her child" - has its origin in the Canon as "a married woman grabs at her baby."

Irene gets to say the line she speaks while in male costume, "Goodnight, Mr Sherlock Holmes," after drugging him in much the same manner as Jeff the cabbie did in the pilot episode. Good thing it was never broadcast, or there'd be no excuse for Sherlock falling for it again.

Holmes' reward at the end of Conan Doyle's story is a photograph of Irene. Here, he takes her camera phone, in spite of the inconvenience to Mycroft and the fact that it's technically evidence. He might, of course, have replaced it with the duplicate he had made to fool Irene earlier in the episode, but evidently chooses not to. Brothers, eh?

Another apparent influence upon Moffat's script is Billy Wilder's 1970 film *The Private Life of Sherlock Holmes*, in which Holmes (Robert Stephens) is bewitched and hoodwinked by Gabrielle Valladon (Genevieve Page), alias German spy Ilse von Hoffmanstal. She is taken into custody by Mycroft Holmes (Christopher Lee), who comments, "You're mush better than most operatives working for British Intelligence." Compare this with "I wish our lot were half as good as you," spoken by Mark Gatiss' Mycroft here. Both co-creators have spoken of their admiration for *Private Life*, and the depiction of Mycroft in this series owes an equal debt to Conan Doyle's original character and to Christopher Lee's interpretation of the role in Wilder's film.

Speaking of Holmes movies, it's impossible not to see a touch of Guy Richie's style in the slo-mo fight sequence with the CIA operatives at Irene's house.

One of John's blog entries is headed *Sherlock Holmes Baffled*, the title of the character's very first film appearance, a short (and boy, do I mean short) from around 1900.

There are, needless to say, numerous references to other tales from the Canon scattered throughout the episode. John christens a case concerning comic books *The Geek Interpreter*, a pun on Mycroft's introductory tale *The Greek Interpreter*. Other slightly altered titles include *The Speckled Blonde* for *The Speckled Band* and *The Navel Treatment* for *The Naval Treaty*.

Moriarty's text to Mycroft - "Dear me, Mr Holmes, Dear

me" - shares its wording with the note sent by a triumphant professor to Holmes the younger at the end of the final novel, *The Valley of Fear*.

Sherlock's website, according to John, differentiates 240 types of tobacco ash (Sherlock corrects him – it's 243). The monograph in which he describes his research is mentioned in *The Boscombe Valley Mystery*, where he's only reached 140 brands – well, he's had over a hundred years to work on it. The *Elementary* episode *A Giant Gun, Filled With Drugs* presents a variation on the same reference.

Once again, Sherlock chides John with the words "You see but do not observe."

Likening the faked terrorist incident to the wartime bombing of Coventry, Sherlock comments, "The wheel turns, nothing is ever new," which is not unlike his observation in *A Study in Scarlet*, "There is nothing new under the sun. It has all been done before."

At Buckingham Palace, Sherlock asks, "And my client is..?" to which the Queen's Equerry replies, "Illustrious." What else could this be but a reference to *The Retired Colourman*? No, wait. Sorry. *The Illustrious Client*. "I'm used to mystery at one end of my cases, both ends is too much," Sherlock complains, just as he did in the original. Why he should consider it a mystery, given that they've been brought to the home of Her Majesty the Queen, and are presently being addressed by her Equerry is, as Mycroft points out, hard to fathom.

Two significant items of attire make their first appearance in *A Scandal in Belgravia*. Sherlock is seen in a dressing gown, the Canonical Holmes' garment of choice for lounging around Baker Street. And then there's the deerstalker, which Sherlock grabs to evade the attention of photographers, accidentally giving himself a trademark look, referenced in all the episodes this season. This item of headgear has long been associated with Sherlock Holmes, and many films have had him wearing it whether in the town or the country. Like Watson's moustache, it's actually an invention of *Strand Magazine* artist Sidney Paget, who first drew Holmes wearing it in *The Boscombe Valley Mystery*. In *Silver Blaze*, Conan Doyle writes that Holmes is wearing "his ear-flapped travelling cap," which Paget again depicted as a deerstalker. Critics have argued for decades over whether or not this was the writer's intention (I happen to think that it was). It's interesting to note that, after Paget's death, the deerstalker vanished from the *Strand* until it resurfaced in Frank Wiles' drawings for the final published story, *Shoscombe Old Place*.

Speaking of the publication that made Holmes famous, Sherlock says he's taken a safety deposit box at a bank on the Strand. Given the degree of detail put into this series, that's probably an intentional nod.

There is, however, something of a missed opportunity in our fist sight of Sherlock's bedroom – in *The Dying Detective*, Conan Doyle notes that the walls are adorned with "pictures of celebrated criminals." Here, it's just the Periodic Table. Who might the 21st Century Sherlock have had in his room? Bernie Madoff? OJ?

Some of Holmes' "missing" cases are name-dropped in this episode, too. The Queen herself enjoyed John's reminiscence about the aluminium crutch. In *The Musgrave Ritual*, this is described as a pre-Watson problem, but we get no further details about it either here or in *The Hounds of Baskerville*, where it is mentioned in passing once again. Conan Doyle has ruined the lives of many a pastiche writer by forcing them to learn more about the properties of aluminium and the behaviour of bees than they would otherwise care to know.

In order to get John to duck when he's about to open Irene's safe and cause the gun within to go off, Sherlock yells "Vatican Cameos!" This is the affair Holmes was preoccupied with in *The Hound of the Baskervilles* at the time of Sir Charles Baskerville's death.

We know about John's army background, but this is the first episode to specify in the dialogue that he belonged to the Fifth Northumberland Fusiliers, as did the Canonical Watson.

He reveals in this story that his middle name is Hamish, and though this is not strictly Canonical, Dorothy L Sayers, the creator of Lord Peter Wimsey, suggested it as an explanation for the fact that Watson's wife calls him James rather than John in *The Man With the Twisted Lip*, Hamish being the Scottish equivalent of James, more or less. Many pastiche writers have taken this as gospel – in *Sherlock Holmes: A Game of Shadows*, Hamish given as the middle name of Jude Law's Watson, too.

Why is the counter on John's blog stuck at 1895? Because Vincent Starrett's poem *221B* ends with these lines:
"Here, though the world explode, these two survive...
And it is always eighteen ninety-five."

I have never loved: We are given a surprising number of hints regarding Holmes' sexual experience, or lack thereof. "Sex doesn't alarm me," he insists. "How would you know?" asks Mycroft. Mrs Hudson has never known Sherlock to be in any kind of romantic relationship. Irene asks him if he's ever "had" anyone. He evades the question. She says that Moriarty refers to him as the Virgin, though he never does so onscreen.

Sherlock has to be brought to Buckingham Palace wearing only a sheet. When he attempts to march out, Mycroft stands on the sheet leaving his brother naked for a moment. A large percentage of *Sherlock*'s viewers pass out from a combination of shock and joy, and hope they haven't missed too much of the episode when they're finally brought round.

Irene, too, is naked, but for a lot longer (though it's all very tastefully shot, dammit). The pious *Daily Mail* ran a large picture of a naked Lara Pulver to remind us all just how arous- I mean outraged we should be.

Irene deduces John's strong feelings for Sherlock, given that he avoided his friend's photogenic nose and teeth when punching him. Once again, he protests that he's not gay. Irene replies that she is.

John thinks he's got lucky when a glamorous woman approaches him on the street, but she's one of Irene's assistants. It's suggested that he watches porn on his laptop – a very convenient and time-effective way to acquire knowledge of women of many nations and three continents. He's been through a string of girlfriends since Sarah. Even he's having difficulty telling them apart, which is why the latest, Jeanette, walks out on him.

Irene changes the ringtone on Sherlock's mobile phone – it's now a sexy moan, though not after this episode.

Sherlock humiliates Molly at Baker Street by deducing that she's seeing a man for whom she has romantic expectations – it's him, of course. At least he apologises for a change.

A seven-per-cent solution: After Sherlock identifies Irene's body, Mycroft offers him a cigarette (low tar), which he accepts. Mycroft warns John and Mrs Hudson, who search the flat for drugs. It's not the first time, either.

A certain unexpected vein of pawky humour: Sherlock: "I dislike being outnumbered, it makes for too much stupid in the room."

Moriarty's phone plays *Stayin' Alive* by the Bee Gees, appropriate in that it precedes his decision not to kill John and Sherlock after all. It's heard again in *The Reichenbach Fall*, just prior to Moriarty's death.

John: "Do you just carry on talking when I'm away?" Sherlock: "I don't know, how often are you away?"

At Buckingham Palace, John asks if they'll be seeing the Queen, at which point, Mycroft strides in. "Apparently, yes," Sherlock responds.

The Queen's Equerry : "People do come to you for help, don't they, Mr Holmes?" Sherlock: "Not to date anyone with a navy."

John: "You don't trust your own secret service?" Mycroft: "Naturally not. They all spy on people for money."

The fight scene between Sherlock and John is comedy gold. "I always hear 'punch me in the face' when you're speaking, but it's usually subtext," the doctor says when asked to provide his friend with convincing injuries. The fight goes a little too far, and Sherlock attempts to call a halt. "I was a soldier," John reminds him, "I killed people." "You were a doctor!" Holmes protests. "I had bad days!" he replies.

John walks in on Sherlock and a naked Irene. "I've missed something, haven't I?"

Another visual gag – a Cluedo board is pinned to the wall, for some reason. We find out a little more about this in the next episode.

My head is in a whirl: A hiker is killed by a stray boomerang? And we're sure this comes under the category of "improbable" rather than "impossible"? Well, OK then.

The extraordinarily cautious Mycroft is extraordinarily careless in discussing the "Bond Air" operation in front of his brother. And how exactly is Flight 007 supposed to "save the world"? Plainly, the terrorist incident in Düsseldorf had no effect. Is Mycroft's plan really to keep blowing up planes until it has the desired effect?

Most important of all, who's the woman on the slab? Her body is an exact match for Irene's – Sherlock, a trained observer, has no hesitation in identifying her corpse as the woman he matched wits with in Belgravia, so this is no spur-of-the-moment substitution. Which begs the question: did Irene murder her? If she did, it makes it a little tough to root for her. If not, how did this poor woman die, and who mutilated her features? Perhaps Moriarty, once again fulfilling the role of Bad Samaritan, provided the cadaver. That doesn't really help matters, though, since it means that he killed an innocent woman and Irene was OK with that.

"All lives end, all hearts are broken. Caring is not an advantage, Sherlock." The script for *A Scandal in Belgravia* is filled with those little touches of wit and invention one expects from Steven Moffat. The visual flourishes are back with a vengeance, including a smart sequence where Sherlock, Irene and Irene's couch are transported to the scene of the hiker's death – an interactive flashback. But for the first time, we have an episode that might have been better with a shorter running length. The pace of story varies drastically from scene to scene, perhaps due in part to the fact that it takes place over a considerable period of time, but needn't. Obviously weeks or even months pass during which Sherlock's reputation builds in those early scenes. Things start to move again once the Irene plotline begins, but then grind to a halt with the unnecessary acknowledgement of the Christmas and New Year festivities. Another six months pass, during which Sherlock has Irene's phone (and the battery still hasn't died – I want one), then at least another two months until news is received of her second "death." Speaking of which, surely no-one really believes Irene is dead when that old mystery movie favourite, a body with a mutilated face is discovered? It's simply a question of marking time until she shows up again. This element really feels like filler, and serves no useful purpose in the storyline.

It would seem from her password and her insistence in her call to Moriarty that he be allowed to live, that Irene has fallen for Sherlock big time without ever actually meeting him. Luckily, her feelings are reciprocated. So, take heart, stalkers of the world: there's hope for you yet.

It's questionable whether Irene would still be of the opinion that brainy is the new sexy if, instead of resembling Benedict Cumberbatch, Holmes looked anything like the author of this book (picture withheld out of sheer human decency).

2X02: The Hounds of Baskerville
UK Airdate: 8 Jan 2012

Writer: Mark Gatiss
Director: Paul McGuigan

Guest Cast: Russell Tovey (Henry Knight); Amelia Bullmore (Dr Stapleton); Clive Mantle (Dr Frankland); Simon Paisley Day (Major Barrymore); Sasha Behar (Dr Mortimer); Will Sharpe (Corporal Lyons); Stephen Wight (Fletcher); Gordon Kennedy (Gary); Kevin Trainor (Billy); Rosalind Knight (Grace); Sam Jones (Young Henry); Chipo Chung (Presenter); Simon Blood DeVay (Scientist)*

*Uncredited

Plot: It's been a whole morning since Sherlock last solved a case, and the only fresh problem presented to him since then comes from little Kirsty, whose rabbit Bluebell turned luminous before vanishing.

Rescue from boredom comes in the form of Henry Knight. He brings with him a fantastic myth from his native land of Dartmoor – the myth of Baskerville Chemical and Biological Weapons Research Centre, rumoured to be creating genetic animal mutations for the battlefield. Henry is certain that, as a child, he saw his father murdered by a huge, furry beast with glowing red eyes. Young Henry was traumatised, his father's body was never discovered. Now, twenty years later, he has returned to the scene of the killing, Dewer's Hollow, where he discovers "the footprints of a gigantic hound!"

They follow their client back to Dartmoor to investigate the case of the dog in the Knight-time. Staying at the Cross Keys Inn, John notices an invoice for supplies of meat, despite their proud boast of a vegetarian menu. The manager, Gary is glad of the income the tale of the demon hound is bringing into the area.

Sherlock questions the local tour guide, Fletcher, who claims to have seen the hound – he, too, believes that the beast is an escaped Baskerville experiment, and has a plaster cast of an enormous paw-print in his rucksack.

Using Mycroft's ID, Sherlock and John are allowed to inspect the Baskerville labs. They meet the genial and very tall Dr Bob Frankland and Dr Stapleton, whose name Sherlock recognises – she's the mother of young Kirsty, owner of the glow-in-the-dark rabbit, Bluebell, one of her experiments. Sherlock and John's deception is ultimately discovered. They are confronted by Major Barrymore, and rescued by Dr Frankland, who insists that Sherlock is indeed Mycroft. As well as being a friend of Henry Knight, Frankland is an admirer of Holmes' work, and a regular reader of Watson's blog.

Henry tells them that, during his sessions with his therapist, Dr Louise Mortimer, he keeps seeing the words "liberty" and "in." Sherlock proposes taking Henry back out on the moor that night in the hopes that the hound, if it exists, will attack him.

During their expedition, Henry explains that his father and Frankland were friends, despite Knight Sr disapproving of the work going on at Baskerville. John is separated from the others when distracted by the repeated flashing of a light, a message in Morse Code – UMQRA. In Dewer's Hollow, both Sherlock and Henry see the hound, though the detective initially denies it.

At the Cross Keys, Sherlock is visibly shaken, and finally confesses to having seen the gigantic hound. John follows up on the Morse Clue, only to discover a different sort of dogging going on – the amorous Mr Selden keeps catching his belt on the car's light-switch, and the mysterious message is entirely unintentional.

Wining and dining Henry's therapist, John tries to find out whether Sherlock might be suffering from the same mental malady as his client. Frankland ruins John's chances of getting into, among other things, Louise Mortimer's good books, by revealing the nature of his relationship with Sherlock Holmes.

The next morning, Holmes tells Henry that he took the case because he was intrigued by his client's use of the archaic term "hound." He runs into Lestrade, who is working undercover on Mycroft's instructions. John tells him about the Inn's order for meat. Gary confesses to keeping a large dog in a nearby mine shaft, hoping to boost tourism. Billy the chef (and Gary's lover) claims that the dog was put down.

While Henry gradually descends into madness, Sherlock and John get Mycroft's authorization to return to Baskerville. John's search for the hound is terrifyingly successful. Having first been disoriented by light and noise, he finds himself trapped in an unlit lab, able to hear the snarling of the fearsome beast before he is finally rescued by Sherlock, who is now certain that, despite the evidence of their eyes, they have both somehow been drugged.

Sherlock remembers Project HOUND, an experiment that took place in Liberty, Indiana (hence Henry's recollection of the words Liberty and In) two decades earlier. Deducing Barrymore's password, he's able to find out the details of the experiment, an attempt to create a delirient drug delivered by aerosol. Bob Frankland has evidently been continuing the experiments.

Convinced that he is being stalked by the hound, Henry fires a gun at Dr Mortimer. John gets a call from the distraught therapist. Lestrade, John and Sherlock catch up with Henry at Dewer's Hollow before he can commit suicide. Sherlock explains that on the night of his father's murder, he didn't see a monster, but Frankland in a gas mask and a HOUND T-shirt. The dog he saw the previous night was an ordinary dog, he insists... but then the hound appears to all of them. Henry shoots it, and as the effects of the drug wear off, they see it for what it is – Gary and Billy's dog, which they couldn't bear to put down. The hallucinations were caused by the fog, actually the gas from the Project HOUND experiments. Frankland is present, too – he's the one who's been gassing Henry in the hope of driving him into madness before he can recall the details of his father's murder. In making his escape from the chemical minefield, Frankland runs into the actual minefield surrounding the Baskerville labs, and is killed.

The case of over, but Sherlock's difficulties are just beginning. At an undisclosed location, Mycroft Holmes has no option but to order the release of James Moriarty, a man with just one thing on his mind...

The best and the wisest man: Sherlock is going stir crazy as the episode begins, not helped by the fact that he's unable to get his hands on any cigarettes – Mycroft's gesture in *A Scandal in Belgravia* evidently caused a relapse. Benedict Cumberbatch seems to be channelling Jeremy Brett in these early scenes. He's written a blog on the identification of perfume and recognises the brand Mrs Hudson is using to drive Mr Chatterjee wild as Casbah Nights. In addition to stealing Lestrade's ID (see *A Study in Pink*), he also has Mycroft's "Access All Areas" pass. He really overdoes it when praising John, perhaps because he's planning to drug him and it's a form of pre-emptive apology. He's able to drive – we see him behind the wheel of a vehicle in Dartmoor. He's genuinely afraid after seeing the hound for the first time, and can't prevent his hands from shaking. He stores memories in his mind palace. He sees Moriarty (the thing he fears the most) when he removes Frankland's gas mask.

I am lost without my Boswell: John regularly e-mails his girlfriends, and Sherlock regularly reads those e-mails. He's hidden Sherlock's cigarettes under his skull (that still sounds odd). He's retained his army ID and uses it when being escorted round the Baskerville labs – he enjoys pulling rank when he gets the chance. He's wearying of Sherlock's habit of turning his coat collar up in order to look cool. He considers himself Sherlock's friend. "I don't have *friends!*" his friend responds. The next day he clarifies his reply, explaining that he has only the one friend, singular. Entirely singular, in fact. He doesn't take sugar in his coffee. John gets to work on his own for a large portion of the episode, but his pursuit of the Morse Code message and his subtle interrogation of Louise Mortimer, both end in humiliation.

The efficiency of our detective police force: Lestrade is just back from a holiday, and boasts a healthy tan. John knows his first name, Greg, but Sherlock has never bothered to find it out. He enjoys working outside London, and has no difficulty getting access to a gun.

There is a strong family resemblance about misdeeds: It's quite surprising that the producers should have waited until the second season before taking a crack at the most famous Sherlock Holmes book, and, after *Dracula*, probably the most-filmed novel of all time. In the Conan Doyle original, Holmes and Watson are tasked with protecting the last member of the Baskerville family, Sir Henry. An ancient legend states that a spectral hound has stalked all the males of the family since Cromwell's time. The hound is shown to be a very real threat, a massive dog coated in a handily unscented phosphorescent paint by Sir Henry's neighbour Jack Stapleton, who turns out to be a previously unknown member of the Baskerville family, out for the inheritance. Given its reputation, it's surprising that Holmes is absent for a large portion of the book.

Several plot elements have been cleverly updated. Sir Henry has been robbed of his title, which becomes his surname. The manuscript bearing the legend of the hound is replaced by a documentary on the secretive experimental site. Part of Fletcher the tour guide's patter, "Stay away from the moor at night if you value your lives," is very similar to the warning letter received by Sir Henry Baskerville: "As you value your life or your reason keep away from the moor." Incidentally, the guide gets his name from Conan Doyle's friend Fletcher Robinson, who provided the writer with the inspiration for the tale.

Many names from *The Hound of the Baskervilles* are recycled, though the characters in this episode bear no resemblance to those in the book. Dr Stapleton proves to be entirely innocent (of anything other than ungodly animal experimentation) while Jack Stapleton was the killer, using his own wife as a lure for the lovesick Henry Baskerville.

Major Barrymore takes his name from Sir Henry's butler, who is receiving messages from a convict hiding out on the moor - his brother-in-law Selden, the Notting Hill Murderer. This aspect of the storyline is briefly acknowledged when John spots what appears to be a message in Morse Code – the romantic soul in the car accidentally signalling with his belt is named Selden.

The Frankland of the novel is no murderer, just a mean-spirited old swine obsessed with litigation. He has a daughter named Laura Lyons with whom he has broken all ties. There's a Corporal Lyons at Baskerville, but absolutely no suggestion of any familial relationship.

Frankland is played by Clive Mantle, who appears briefly in the 1988 Sherlock Holmes comedy *Without a Clue*, starring Michael Caine and Ben Kingsley.

Holmes and Watson's client in *The Hound of the Baskervilles* is Dr James Mortimer, a local physician and friend of the Baskerville family. Louise Mortimer has at least some ties to Henry Knight, but is otherwise entirely unlike her namesake.

The Great Grimpen Mire, the swamp which (probably) claims the life of the evil Stapleton has been cleverly reimagined as the Great Grimpen Minefield, which claims the life of the evil Frankland. Gary and Billy keep their phoney hound chained up in an abandoned mineshaft, just as Jack Stapleton did.

Sherlock's assessment of the case as "refined, cold-blooded murder" can be found in Chapter 12 of the novel. Elsewhere, he says of John, "You've never been the most luminous of people, but as a conductor of light, you are unbeatable. Some people who aren't geniuses have an amazing ability to stimulate it in others." This is an almost direct quote from the first chapter, and can also be heard in the *Elementary* episode *A Landmark Story*.

The substance Sherlock craves that is seven-per-cent stronger than tea, is, of course, cocaine. The oft-quoted dosage is mentioned just once, in *The Sign of Four*.

In his quest for cigarettes, he briefly checks a slipper for traces of cigarettes. In *The Musgrave Ritual*, Holmes notes that Holmes keeps his tobacco "in the toe end of a Persian Slipper."

Sherlock first appears in this episode clutching a harpoon, and drenched with blood. The story *Black Peter* begins in much the same way, although the Holmes of the Canon thinks his experiment worthwhile rather than "tedious."

His claim that his brother Mycroft "practically *is* the

British Government" has its origins in *The Bruce-Partington Plans*.

In *A Study in Scarlet*, Stamford tells Watson that he could imagine Holmes giving a friend a pinch of a vegetable alkaloid "in order to have an accurate idea of the effects." In fact, Sherlock only thinks he's drugging John by placing sugar in his coffee – it later transpires that John has inhaled some of the gas from leaking pipes at the facility – but he's still happy to take advantage of it and throw the doctor into a state of blind panic. Small wonder he has only one friend.

The term Sherlock uses to describe the suntanned Lestrade - "as brown as a nut" - is the same one used by Stamford when meeting Watson for the first time following his return from Afghanistan.

Fletcher the tour guide is tricked into showing off his cast of the hound's print when Sherlock gives the impression that he has a bet with John, the same strategy employed by Holmes in *The Blue Carbuncle* when attempting to track down the seller of a Christmas goose containing a stolen gem.

Fletcher's friend in the MOD claims to have seen rats as big as dogs in the labs. Might this be a reference to Holmes' most famous missing case, the Giant Rat of Sumatra?

Henry's belief that a man in a gas mask was in fact a hideous creature mirrors *The Masks of Death*, starring Peter Cushing and John Mills as Holmes and Watson. In the 1984 film, a drunken beggar sees German spies sporting gas masks, and thinks them pig-like creatures.

"I envy you so much," he tells John. "Your mind, it's so placid, straightforward, barely used." This is the second reference in two weeks to Billy Wilder's *The Private Life of Sherlock Holmes*. The very next line, in which he likens his own mind to "an engine, racing out of control," is a variation on a quote from *Wisteria Lodge*, and is also placed in the mouth of Robert Downey Jr in his first Holmes movie.

In Dr Stapleton's lab, we see a monkey apparently giving a Nazi salute, echoing the cheeky monkey in *Raiders of the Lost Ark* (I've had some bad dates, but most of them involved her pouring a drink in my lap and telling me never to call again).

While recovering from their first excursion to Dewer's Hollow, John calls Sherlock "Spock," referring not to the child psychologist but to the emotionless Vulcan from TV's *Star Trek*. In the motion picture *Star Trek VI: The Undiscovered Country*, written and directed by *Seven-Per-Cent Solution* author Nicholas Meyer, Mr Spock (Leonard Nimoy) states that he is a descendant of Sherlock Holmes. Zachary Quinto's Spock also quotes Holmes in the highly successful 2009 reboot.

The inspiration for the mind palace to which Holmes retreats in order to recover the information on HOUND might well be Thomas Harris' 1999 novel *Hannibal*.

Billy the chef buys the food for the *faux* hound from Undershaw Meat Supplies, named for Conan Doyle's Surrey home. Mark Gatiss is patron of the Undershaw Preservation Trust.

For some reason, Gatiss has first Sherlock and then John say "I've not been idle" in both his scripts, but if the phrase originates somewhere other than in the author's imagination, I'm really not sure. Something for the Second Edition, maybe.

I have never loved: John's given up on explaining that he and Sherlock aren't gay, even when Gary at the Cross Keys apologises for not being able to provide them with a double room. Frankland probably gives Louise Mortimer the wrong impression about John's preferences when she describes him as Sherlock's "live-in PA."

A seven-per-cent solution: Sherlock has paid off everyone in a two-mile radius not to sell him cigarettes. He complains that he needs something "seven-per-cent stronger" than tea. He later encourages Henry Knight to smoke.

A certain unexpected vein of pawky humour: Sherlock tries to persuade John to tell him where his secret stash of ciggies is kept in return for next week's lottery numbers – even he knows it's preposterous.

John refuses to play Cluedo again with Sherlock, who insisted during their last game that the victim did it, and the rules of the board game are therefore wrong.

John: "In your own time." Sherlock: "But quite quickly."

John attempts to sympathise with Henry, but it's far from easy with Sherlock noisily inhaling their client's cigarette smoke.

Dr Stapleton: "I have a lot of fingers in a lot of pies. I like to mix things up – genes, mostly. Now and again, actual fingers."

My head is in a whirl: So why did Frankland kill Henry's dad? It's the issue at the heart of the story, but it's barely acknowledged. Henry suggests that his father had "found something out." How vague is that? In addition, Frankland's explosive end means we never find out what he did with the body, either.

Why does Sherlock switch from saying he won't be accompanying John to Dartmoor, to saying that he will mere seconds later? Of course, it's a fakeout – in the novel, Sherlock claims he can't go with John and Sir Henry Baskerville, but is, in fact, observing events from a nearby hut on the moor. Even so, the abrupt change of mind makes no sense in this context.

Listeners to the popular BBC Radio 2 morning show hosted by Chris Evans wondered just where Sherlock and John acquired the jeep they use in Dartmoor – presumably, they loaned it from Henry.

It seems out of character for the professionally mistrustful Mycroft to think nothing of the fact that his security pass is missing, the one that affords access to all government facilities. No harm in that falling into the wrong hands, surely?

Pity the producers couldn't afford the voice of the real Elvis – even from a few short words, it's plainly not the King himself.

It's astonishing that Lestrade simply takes Gary and Billy's word for it that they had their dog destroyed. How hard would it have been for him to phone the vet and confirm it?

Billy complains about "the ruddy prisoner." But what prisoner? There's an escaped prisoner in Conan Doyle's story, but nowhere in this episode! He's not referring to Mycroft's incarceration of Moriarty, is he? Maybe Billy knows far more than he's telling.

Just a small point, but why does the lady enjoying Selden's company address him as "*Mr* Selden"? In all other respects, they seem quite close.

"Twenty year-old disappearance? A Monstrous hound? I wouldn't miss this for the world!" Scriptwriter Mark Gatiss is evidently trying for a modern Hammer Horror-vibe with *The Hounds of Baskerville*, but the lack of a through-line in the plot robs it of much of its potential for suspense – Sherlock and John have to visit every location twice before any progress can be made. The absence of a motive for the killer, surely one of the prerequisites of the mystery genre, is deeply unsatisfying.

It's almost as though *Sherlock* has gone meta – Frankland is the murderer, not for any particular reason but because the series requires that *someone* be the murderer. It's the second near-miss in two episodes, both from the writers of the standout entries in Season One. Scenes of Henry descending into madness seem to go on for ages. Gatiss modestly gives himself only one line of dialogue as Mycroft (who, of course, doesn't appear in the original novel). When finally seen, the hound in this story looks as phoney as the one in the last BBC adaptation ten years earlier, but given that its appearance is largely imaginary, that might well be the point.

2X03: The Reichenbach Fall
UK Airdate: 15 January 2012

Writer: Steve Thompson
Director: Toby Haynes

Guest Cast: Katherine Parkinson (Kitty Riley); Tanya Moodie (Ella); Tony Pitts (Chief Superintendent); Jaye Griffiths (Prosecuting Barrister); Ian Hallard (Defence Barrister); Malcolm Rennie (Judge); Sydney Wade (Claudie Bruhl); Edward Holtom (Max Bruhl); Paul Leonard (Bank Director); Christopher Hunter (Prison Governor); Tony Way (Prison Warder); Lorraine Hilton (Miss Mackenzie); Samantha-Holly Bennett (Reporter #1); Peter Basham (Reporter #2); Rebecca Noble (Reporter #3); Robert Benfield (Gallery Director); Ifan Huw Dafydd (Clerk of the Court); Michael Mueller (Father); Pano Masti (Assassin); Douglas Wilmer (Diogenes Gent); Stuart Mulcaster (Camera Man); Michael Wisniewski (CPS Solicitor); William Charles (Waiter)*; Gillian Steventon (Nurse)*; Sy Turner (Paparazzi Photographer)*

*Uncredited

Plot: Sherlock's fame increases with his recovery of the missing Turner masterpiece *Falls of the Reichenbach*, the rescue of a kidnapped banker and the capture of the notorious Peter Ricoletti.

Fearing that the press will inevitably turn on him, John suggests that Sherlock keep a low profile for a while, but that proves impossible when Jim Moriarty, posing as a tourist, visits the Tower of London to inspect the Crown Jewels. Simply by pressing the icons on his mobile phone, Moriarty unlocks the case protecting the Crown Jewels, the vaults at the Bank of England and the cells at Pentonville Prison. When the security guards reach him, he is sat on a throne, draped in ermine, waiting for them to arrest him. He has already sent Sherlock a text, inviting him to "come and play."

Six weeks later, Sherlock is called as an expert witness at Moriarty's sensational trial, shunning the attentions of journalist Kitty Riley, who attempts to get close to him by posing as a groupie. Moriarty does not offer any defence at his trial. It takes the jury six minutes to reach a verdict of *not* guilty.

Sherlock is already waiting as his adversary arrives at Baker Street. Moriarty freely admits to threatening each member of the jury via the televisions in their hotel rooms. Sherlock has deduced that Moriarty's very public crimes were simply a demonstration of his ultimate weapon – a key code capable of accessing any computer program anywhere in the world, effectively ending privacy, secrecy and security forever. The trial was, in effect, an advertisement for his services.

Two months after the acquittal, John is brought to Mycroft's club, the Diogenes. Mycroft advises him that spurned journalist Kitty Riley has, with the assistance of an informant named Richard Brook, written an article for *The Sun* which will apparently reveal "the shocking truth" about Sherlock Holmes. He's also learned that four international assassins have all moved into Baker Street.

At the doorstep of 221B, John finds an envelope filled with breadcrumbs. He doesn't get a chance to tell Sherlock about it, though; Lestrade and Donovan are already present, having brought the kidnapping of the children of US Ambassador Bruhl to the consultant's attention.

Visiting the school from which the children were abducted, Sherlock discovers that Bruhl's son, Max, has left them a trail in linseed oil. John notices that an envelope containing a book of fairy tales found in the daughter's trunk bears a wax seal matching the one on the envelope found outside Baker Street. Sherlock thinks that Moriarty is suggesting the story of Hansel and Gretel to them, and hopes that traces of the sole of the kidnapper's shoe will lead them to the witch's house. With the help of the Homeless Network, he identifies the building in which the children are being held – a disused sweet factory in Addlestone. The children are rescued just in time - the wrappers of the sweets with which they have been fed are coated in mercury.

When Sherlock attempts to interview the girl, Claudette, she points at him and screams. For some reason, he reminds her of her kidnapper. Sally suggests to Lestrade that Sherlock himself engineered the kidnapping. Anderson is quick to back her up. On a cab ride home, Moriarty reveals to Sherlock that this has been his plan – he will burn the detective by destroying his reputation. The Chief Superintendent orders Lestrade to bring Sherlock in for questioning.

Rescued from a near-accident by a man in the street, Sherlock is stunned to see his rescuer shot dead by a sniper. John recognises the dead man as one of the assassins Mycroft warned him about. It would seem that they all believe Sherlock has something of value, but any one of them who approaches him to retrieve it will be killed by the others. The problem is, Sherlock doesn't know what that something is supposed to be.

Sherlock is about to be arrested for kidnapping, but he and John flee. They meet up with another assassin who, at gunpoint, tells them that Moriarty planted the computer key code somewhere in the flat. He doesn't get to elaborate before he, too, is killed.

Sherlock and John visit Kitty to ask about her source, Rich Brook. When Brook appears, they're stunned to see that he's Moriarty. Kitty believes Rich is an actor hired by Sherlock to play a criminal mastermind in order to appear more brilliant, even to the extent of arranging his arrest and trial, on the understanding that Sherlock would rig the jury.

Having worked out the last phase of Moriarty's plan, Sherlock leaves John and seeks out Molly at Bart's. He needs her help: "You've always counted and I've always trusted you," he tells her.

John confronts Mycroft at the Diogenes – he's the only one who could have supplied so much information about Sherlock's background for Kitty's story. Is he conspiring with Moriarty against his own brother? Mycroft admits he had Moriarty interrogated for weeks in the hope that he would give up the location of the key code, but he would talk only to Mycroft, and then only about Sherlock.

Sherlock invites his enemy to meet him on the roof of Bart's. John is drawn away by a call informing him that Mrs Hudson has been shot. But when he gets back to Baker Street, she's alive and well.

In their rooftop confrontation, Moriarty confesses that he's been searching for distractions all his life, and though Sherlock served as the best distraction, now he's been beaten, there's nothing left. Sherlock has finally realised where the key code is hidden – it's inside his head. He memorised it when watching Moriarty drum his fingers during their encounter at Baker Street. But the Napoleon of Crime has a trump card yet to play – there is no computer code, all his break-ins were accomplished with the assistance of accomplices. Now that Sherlock has been so utterly beaten, the only thing remaining is his suicide. The remaining three gunmen will kill John, Mrs Hudson and Lestrade if he doesn't jump from the roof. Moriarty is the only man who can call them off, and he shoots himself rather than be put in a position where he's forced to do so.

Now there's only one way for Sherlock to save his friends...

Standing on the ledge, he phones John, who's just arriving at Bart's. Sherlock "confesses" to being a fake, to inventing Moriarty and stage-managing his investigations. The call is his suicide note, he says. John watches in horror as Sherlock jumps. He's knocked over by a solitary cyclist before he can reach the body as it lands close to a truck loaded with plastic bags, which sets off again just as John reaches his friend. A quick check of his pulse shows that Sherlock's heart is no longer beating. The body is whisked away by hospital staff. In the moments following Sherlock's death, all three assassins stand down.

Visiting Sherlock's grave, John finally gets to express his feelings. He refuses to believe that Sherlock's life was a lie. "I was so alone... and I owe you so much." He asks for one more miracle, that his friend not be dead. But his request goes unanswered, and he turns away to rejoin Mrs Hudson in the waiting taxi, not spotting Sherlock Holmes watching him from a safe distance.

The best and the wisest man: In addition to involving himself in current crimes, Sherlock also solves the mystery surrounding the death of Henry Fishguard, the story of which is relating in an extremely dusty old tome. He's never enjoyed riddles, he claims. That seems unlikely, frankly. Mycroft says there is too much history between the two of them for him to warn his brother about the hitmen living feet away from him. Molly notes that Sherlock looks sad when he imagines John's not looking. Kitty Riley's newspaper article contains a great deal of information about Sherlock's background. A pity we never get to read it, or hear any of it read aloud. As Molly is working, Sherlock uncharacteristically plays with a rubber ball. This is really the turning-point for Cumberbatch's

Sherlock Holmes. Previously, he's left issues of morality to John, being more interested in the prospect of a puzzle than the protection of the innocent. It took him a series and a half to admit that he has even one friend. Now, in addition to realising that he can no longer manipulate Molly Hooper but must treat her as a feeling human being, he is placed in a position where he must make an enormous sacrifice in order to save the lives of the three most important people in his life.

I am lost without my Boswell: Following Sherlock's "death," John sees his therapist Ella for the first time in eighteen months. This doesn't necessarily mean that only eighteen months has passed since *A Study in Pink* – given that *A Scandal in Belgravia* takes up the good part of a year and the scene with the therapist is set three months after the recovery of the Turner painting, it'd be surprising if that were the case. More likely, John continued with his sessions for some time after he moved into Baker Street. John has friends on the force – he receives a warning that Sherlock is to be brought in for questioning. He chins the Chief Superintendent for calling Sherlock a weirdo.
His movements are very military as he turns from Sherlock's grave. It goes without saying that Martin Freeman is excellent – when is he ever not? But when working opposite Benedict Cumberbatch, who's giving it his all on a hospital rooftop prior to taking the ultimate step, he more than holds his own, in a beautifully understated manner.

The efficiency of our detective police force: Once again, Lestrade seems genuinely proud of Sherlock, but isn't beyond embarrassing him, which is why he presents the consulting detective with a deerstalker hat at the Ricoletti press conference. Like Claudette, he feels like screaming when Sherlock walks into a room. He calls him CSI: Baker Street.

Anderson is summoned to St Aldate's school, mostly so that Sherlock can compliment him on his "brilliant impression of an idiot." He's noticeably aggravated when Sherlock makes a comment about bribery. At least his haircut has improved.

Sally Donovan is the first one to experience doubt over Sherlock's results following the kidnapping. She considers his deductions "unbelievable," but not in a good way.

There is a strong family resemblance about misdeeds: There is, by necessity, very little of the story of *The Final Problem* in *The Reichenbach Fall*, since there's very little story in the original. Watson (and by extension) the readers have never heard of Holmes' arch-enemy Professor Moriarty before this tale, which happens to concern the dismantling of his criminal organization. Holmes and Watson go on the run to Switzerland, only for the Professor to catch up with his old enemy at the Reichenbach Falls. Watson is drawn away, but returns to discover the aftermath of a struggle in which both Holmes and Moriarty have presumably fallen to their deaths. As is well-recorded, Conan Doyle intended this to be the final Sherlock Holmes story, though it's hard not to suspect that he at least considered the possibility of reviving his creation at some point (otherwise, why not have Watson witness his friend's death?). So all that remains of *The Final Problem* is the title repeatedly referenced in Jim Moriarty's dialogue, a sly reference to the place of Holmes' mock death, both in the painting and in Moriarty's alias Richard Brook (the German for Reichenbach), the way in which John is drawn away from the climactic confrontation believing that a woman is desperately unwell and, of course, the fall. There's also a précis of

Sherlock's description of Moriarty as "a spider at the centre of a web, a criminal web with a thousand threads, and he knows precisely how each and every single one of them dances." The original wording can be heard in the penultimate *Elementary* episode, *The Woman*. Watson's epitaph for Sherlock Holmes, "The best and the wisest man whom I have ever known," finds modern form as "You were the best man and the most human human being that I've ever known." (Note to self: That "best & wisest man" thing is pretty catchy – try to work it in elsewhere, if possible.)

The episode features another *Empty House* reference – the second or third, depending on whether you count the pilot episode - in the fact that a Russian hitwoman is living in the flat opposite 221B (it must have had extensive repairs since *The Great Game*).

The abduction of the American Ambassador's children suggests *The Priory School* (and, perhaps, an incident in Laurie R King's famous 1994 pastiche novel *The Beekeeper's Apprentice* where the daughter of an American Senator is snatched), and the manner in which Sherlock follows the linseed oil footprints mirrors the pursuit of Jonathan Small and his pygmy accomplice Tonga in *The Sign of Four*. John insults Sherlock by referring to him as a machine, just as Watson did in that second novel: "You really are an automaton – a calculating machine."

Another of the missing cases, Ricoletti of the club foot and his abominable wife, is covered too, with Sherlock's capture of the elusive Peter Ricoletti, who might or might not be single and might or might n- well, you get the idea.

The *Guardian* article on Moriarty's trial name-checks Holmes' creator: "In a twist worthy of a Conan Doyle novella, Mr Sherlock Holmes..."

Probably the episode's greatest coup is the presence at

the Diogenes club of Douglas Wilmer, star of the BBC's 1965 Sherlock Holmes series, opposite Nigel Stock's Watson. These programmes are available on DVD in the States, but aggravatingly, not in the UK. Wilmer also appears briefly as the detective in the 1975 Gene Wilder comedy *The Adventures of Sherlock Holmes' Smarter Brother*, and features in the James Bond film *Octopussy* with Roger Moore. Moore famously contacted Mark Gatiss via Twitter to recommend himself for a role in *Sherlock*. Might he be the second former Holmes to make an appearance in the series?

As stated elsewhere in this book, the notion that Moriarty is an invention of Sherlock Holmes is an idea that's been used before, but Thompson cleverly subverts the concept by having the man himself pretend that he's a fiction.

Moriarty's break-in at the Tower of London is yet another nod to the Rathbone movie *The Adventures of Sherlock Holmes* in which the Professor (George Zucco) almost gets away with the crown jewels. Sherlock's Moriarty, of course, isn't actually interested in getting away. The music he's listening to on his stereo is, fittingly, Gioachino Rossini's *La gazza ladra* (*The Thieving Magpie*).

I have never loved: It's pointed out to John that he is described as "confirmed bachelor John Watson" in the *Daily Star*. "What the hell are they implying?" he asks (the term is repeated in another article following Moriarty's Tower of London coup).

Kitty asks whether the relationship between Sherlock and John is just platonic.

John glances at Kitty as she joins him in the gallery. Given the comedic skills of both Freeman and Katherine Parkinson (the first female Doctor Who – not yet, but mark my words...), there's a sitcom waiting to happen there.

Moriarty calls Sherlock "honey." Make of that what you will.

Molly insists that she and Jim only went out three times. Bearing in mind what occurred after the break-up, Sherlock recommends that she avoid future attempts at a relationship.

Fleeing the police hand-in-hand (having been handcuffed), John remarks, "Now people will definitely talk!"

Molly: "What do you need?" Sherlock: "You." It's a long time 'til morning...

A certain unexpected vein of pawky humour: Sherlock imagines that he might throw his deerstalker at opponents, like some kind of "death Frisbee."

At Moriarty's trial, Sherlock is told by the judge that any "showing off" will be treated as contempt. He opens his mouth to reply, and we jump to a scene of him being led into the cell.

Otherwise, not a lot of laughs in an episode ending with the title character's suicide.

My head is in a whirl: The newspaper article on the kidnapping of the banker doesn't even bother to mention his name (although we'll all be very surprised if it doesn't turn out to be Crosby).

Sherlock is absolutely certain that Moriarty is behind the kidnapping of the Bruhl children, but why? The name never comes up until he and John encounter Molly at the lab, and even at that point, the connection between the envelopes hasn't been noticed.

The Chief Superintendent is astonished to discover that Lestrade has used Sherlock on several "proper" cases. So he doesn't read the papers, then. Or watch the news. Or visit Scotland Yard.

As with the other two entries in this season, there's an important plot point that goes unexplored: Why does Claudette Bruhl scream when she sees Sherlock? This is the turning-point of the episode, the moment where the tide of opinion turns against our hero, so it's a big deal, and yet it's barely addressed. Sherlock sees Moriarty on several occasions after this incident, but never thinks to ask him how he managed it. Even John points out that it makes no sense, and who am I to argue?

"Every fairy tale needs a good old-fashioned villain."
Having scripted the least memorable episode of Season One, Steve Thompson comes up with easily the best entry in the second season. The story keeps its momentum, and the sense of inevitable tragedy pervades every scene. The writer makes full use of all the toys at his disposal this time round, having a map of London visible only to Sherlock, on which he locates the chocolate factory in which the Bruhl children are being held. Of particular brilliance, though, is the decision to show Sherlock alive in the episode's closing moments. Like Irene Adler's phoney demise in *A Scandal in Belgravia*, it's no surprise to learn that he survived, the question is how? The levels of fan excitement reached with this episode will surely be tough to reach ever again, but I have faith.

Part Two: Sherlock Holmes in New York...

...was the title of a 1976 TV movie starring Roger Moore and Patrick Macnee, but that's a story for another time. In the January of 2012, the CBS network – home of the all-powerful *CSI* franchise – announced that their Fall schedule would include *Elementary*, a mystery series in which Sherlock Holmes sets up shop in modern day New York.

Obviously, it would be foolish to suggest that no connection exists between the commissioning of *Elementary* and the runaway success of the BBC's show. In fact, Sue Vertue, executive producer of *Sherlock* stated in an interview with the *Independent* that CBS had initially approached the production company Hartswood Films about remaking the programme. "We are very proud of our show," she said, "and like any proud parent, will protect the interest and well-being of our offspring." So fingers crossed this book doesn't make things worse.

It's likely that CBS chose to go their own way because of the public domain status of the source material, and because several US TV shows of recent vintage have drawn their inspiration from the Canon, particularly *Monk* and *House* (Hollywood execs, keep an eye out for my forthcoming spec script, *Monkhouse*). It would be insane not to exploit the original tales at some point, and what better time than with one Sherlock Holmes riding high at the box office and another enjoying strong ratings and uniformly positive reviews across the pond? The situation is not unlike the famous Battle of the Bonds, with Roger Moore's *Octopussy* and Sean Connery's *Never Say Never Again* being released within months of each other.

This wouldn't be the first that Holmes has been seen in the modern day America – the TV movies *The Return of Sherlock Holmes* and *Sherlock Holmes Returns* (starring

Michael Pennington and Anthony Higgins respectively) both had the detective revived from suspended animation and resuming his career Stateside.

But nor is this the first series called *Elementary* written for US television. In 2000, nine years before *Sherlock*'s pilot episode began shooting, scriptwriter Josh Friedman – presently co-writing *Avatar 2* with James Cameron – penned a pilot script entitled *Elementary*, based in present day San Francisco.

The storyline is a pretty close adaptation of *The Musgrave Ritual* (the subject of another updating in the 1943 Basil Rathbone picture *Sherlock Holmes Faces Death*) and features an American Holmes and Watson, both male, who are on first-name terms. Sherlock favours the piano to the violin, and Watson is a former psychiatrist, struck off following an affair with a female patient.

Friedman litters the script with references to the Canon in general: the presence of Lestrade, the brief appearance of a *fat* Mycroft, mention of Holmes beating corpses with a golf club in order to establish bruising after death, and somewhere in the background, the baleful influence of Moriarty. Almost prophetically, Watson declares "I believe in Sherlock", and onscreen subtitles are used not to establish location but to relay relevant plot information to the viewer.

The story is told as a flashback from Watson's perspective following his arrest for the murder of none other than- Well, perhaps it's unfair to go into too much detail. Had it ever been filmed, the script might well have undergone many changes. In fact, who's to say that it won't ever be filmed? Just because it seems improbable doesn't mean it's impossible. Friedman obviously intended certain plot threads to be pursued over a number of episodes, and it's a shame that we might never find out just what he had in mind for *Elementary* Mk 1.

It may be that there's no direct connection between Friedman's script and the show devised by Robert Doherty for CBS. Stranger coincidences have occurred – for instance, two entirely different comic strip characters called *Dennis the Menace* appeared in the US and the UK on the very same day, the 12th of March 1951, without any collusion between the creators or the slightest hint of plagiarism. Indeed, the title and contemporary setting aside, there's little real similarity between the two *Elementary*s.

Robert Doherty's version focuses on an aspect of the detective's life that, while undoubtedly important, merits little more than a paragraph in Conan Doyle's *The Missing Three-Quarter*: namely, his recovery from "that drug mania which had threatened once to check his remarkable career." This series, therefore begins with Holmes having checked out of rehab and finding himself lumbered with a sober companion, former Dr Joan Watson, who must accompany him on all his investigations in order to ensure that he remains drug-free.

Many die-hard *Sherlock* fans smell conspiracy in the casting of Jonny Lee Miller in the lead role. Miller had earlier starred alongside Benedict Cumberbatch in an acclaimed stage adaptation of *Frankenstein*. By the same logic, CBS came perilously close to casting a CGI horse as Holmes.

Appearing alongside Miller is former *Ally McBeal* and *Charlie's Angels* star Lucy Liu as Joan Watson. Liu is not the first female Watson, by any means. Joanne Woodward was psychologist Dr Mildred Watson opposite George C Scott in the 1971 film *They Might be Giants* (the first motion picture to collapse under the weight of its own whimsy), Margaret Colin played Jane Watson in *The Return of Sherlock Holmes* and Debrah Farentino, though her character is named Dr Amy Winslow, fulfilled the same function in *Sherlock Holmes Returns*.

Elementary was no moderate success for CBS – Episode Fourteen, *The Deductionist*, was selected to follow the 2013 Superbowl (a big deal for any network show) and the first season's run was extended from 22 to 24 episodes, a notable achievement in an era when budget restraints mean that many programmes manage only 17 or so instalments.

Looking back, I now realise that I should've called this section of the book "It's Miller Time!" Too late now. Damn.

ELEMENTARY
CBS

Creator: Robert Doherty

Executive Producers: Robert Doherty, Carl Beverly, Sarah Timberman, Craig Sweeny & Michael Cuesta

Music: Sean Callery, Zoe Keating

Regular Cast: Jonny Lee Miller (Sherlock Holmes); Lucy Liu (Joan Watson); Aidan Quinn (Captain Tobias Gregson); Jon Michael Hill (Detective Marcus Bell); Stephen Park (Oren Watson); Vinnie Jones (Sebastian Moran); Natalie Dormer (Irene Adler); Linda Emond (Dr Candace Reed); Ato Essandoh (Alfredo Llamosa); Kristine Johnson (TV Reporter); Michael Iannucci (Medical Examiner); Erik Jensen (Isaac Proctor)

Jon Michael Hill appears in episodes 2-24 only
Stephen Park appears in Episodes 10 and 24 only - in the latter, he is uncredited
Vinnie Jones appears in episodes 12 and 21 only
Natalie Dormer appears in episodes 22-24 only
Linda Emond appears in episodes 12, 13 and 16 only
Ato Essandoh appears in episodes 6, 18 and 20 only
Kristine Johnson appears in episodes 21 and 22 only
Michael Iannucci appears in episodes 23 and 24 only
Erik Jensen appears in episodes 23 and 24 only

1X01: Pilot
US Airdate: 27 September 2012

Writer: Robert Doherty
Director: Michael Cuesta

Guest Cast: Dallas Roberts (Dr Richard Mantlo); Manny Perez (Detective Javier Abreu); Jonathan Walker (Harrison Polk); Kristen Bush (Eileen Renfro); Craig Walker (Peter Saldua); Michael Nathanson (Infomercial Narrator); Randal Turner (Male Opera Singer); Melissa Zapin (Female Opera Singer); Sherry H Arell (Shushing Lady); Annika Boras (Amy Damper)*; Ward Horton (Soap Opera Actor)*; Roy Pollack (NYC Pedestrian)*

*Uncredited

Plot: Joan Watson's first day as sober companion to Sherlock Holmes does not go as expected. Holmes, a consultant with the NYPD, leads her to the home of psychiatrist Dr Richard Mantlo, who has notified the police following the disappearance of his wife, Amy Dampier. Following an examination of a struggle in the couple's home, Holmes leads Captain Gregson to Amy's dead body in the safe room.

Holmes and Watson speak to a Dr Harrison Polk, a friend of the Mantlos, who confirms that Amy underwent a good deal of unnecessary plastic surgery.

Holmes suspects that the killer may have struck before. He tracks down Eileen Renfrow, who is physically similar to Amy, and managed to survive an attack by the same man. Annoyed by Holmes' bombastic approach, she later admits to Watson that she knew her attacker, Peter Saldua, who now works for a florist in Chelsea. But Saldua is dead, an apparent suicide. His cell phone is missing from his home. It's learned that Saldua delivered fresh flowers to the Mantlo house every week and that he'd been seeing a psychologist, Dr Jessop, who died of a heart attack two years earlier.

Holmes suspects that Dr Mantlo took over Saldua's treatment from Jessop, provided his patient with steroids in order to increase his aggression levels, and pressured his wife into having plastic surgery, thus making her more like Saldua's preferred victim type. Frustrated by the lack of evidence and Mantlo's insistence that he never knew or treated Saldua, Holmes drives Watson's car into the psychiatrist's own vehicle and winds up in jail. While he is locked up, Watson is struck by the presence of a large bag of rice in Saldua's home, despite his allergies. Holmes deduces that Saldua accidentally put his cellphone in the washing machine, and subsequently placed it in the bag of rice in an attempt to dry it out. Saldua recorded all his sessions with Mantlo on his phone, and now that it is functioning again, Gregson has enough evidence to charge him.

The Best and the wisest man: Holmes first appears shirtless, practising a memory game which involves watching several television recordings simultaneously (we see him do this again in *The Long Fuse* and *Dirty Laundry*). His father owns five properties in New York, a fact that becomes relevant in the episode *M*. He considers the brownstone in which he lives to be the shoddiest of all the residences. The address of the brownstone still has yet to be revealed at the end of Season One. He tells Watson that he often gets bored. He uses Google when his deductive abilities fail him. He refers to the New York subway system as "the tube." He insists that he doesn't really care for opera, even though his father thinks he's a buff. This may well be an example of Holmes' resentment for his unseen and unnamed parent, since he knows when a singer is off-key. He has no mirrors in his home. Watson suggests that Holmes knows a lost cause when he sees one.

I am lost without my Boswell: Joan Watson was once a surgeon, but made a mistake during surgery which cost a patient their life. No specific details of this tragedy have been revealed thus far, and the name of the patient has never been stated. She still visits his grave in Culver Cemetery. Abandoning medicine, she became a sober companion. Her services have been secured by Holmes' father for six weeks, meaning that she and Sherlock investigate roughly two cases per week until she is forced to make a decision regarding her future in *M*. In this episode, she addresses her charge as "Mr Holmes;" for the rest of the series, she calls him "Sherlock". She has two alarm clocks, because getting up is such a chore. Watson has a car, but it's never seen after Holmes smashes it up (in *The Red Team*, she's driving a rental). To paraphrase *Futurama*, nobody drives in New York because there's too much traffic. She's a baseball fan, though this never crops up again. In fairness, the Canonical Watson's fondness for rugby is rarely mentioned either. Like Martin Freeman, Lucy Liu has decided to play Watson without a moustache. A wise choice – it's not a look that would suit either of them.

The efficiency of our detective police force: Captain Toby (?) Gregson first met Holmes when the American was observing counter-terrorism procedures in London. Holmes has deduced his password for the NYPD website. He likes to hang out in an Irish pub.

Detective Javier Abreu makes his one and only

appearance in this episode. His role and characteristics are transferred to Detective Bell in the very next episode.

There is a strong family resemblance about misdeeds: Holmes' observations regarding the lack of symmetry in Mantlo's living room recall not a Holmes tale, but G K Chesterton's Father Brown mystery *The Worst Crime in the World*.

In Conan Doyle's *His Last Bow*, the retired Holmes has written a book entitled *Practical Handbook of Bee Culture, With Some Observations Upon the Segregation of the Queen*. The CBS Sherlock keeps a hive of bees on the roof (honey drips through the ceiling sometimes). He's writing a book with the same title, but it exists entirely in his mind – he's reached Chapter 19.

Captain Gregson shares his name with Inspector Tobias Gregson, who appears in *A Study in Scarlet*, *The Greek Interpreter* and *The Red Circle*. Holmes considered him "the smartest of the Scotland Yarders." By the next episode, Gregson's forename has changed to Thomas.

I have never loved: Watson sees a prostitute leaving the brownstone as she arrives. Holmes insists that he finds sex repellent but feeds the need as his body requires it. Watson doesn't believe him, but future episodes seem to bear out his claim.

A seven-per-cent solution: Holmes has been confined at Hemdale Rehabilitation Facility, but escaped shortly before he was due to be released. He watched baseball games with the other inmates at Hemdale.

He tells Watson he's finished with drugs, though the temptation he's placed under later in the season suggests that this is wishful thinking on his part.

Watson conducts a saliva test on Holmes after he

unplugs her alarm clocks in order to ditch her.

A certain unexpected vein of pawky humour: Most of the comedy in *Elementary* revolves around Holmes' ability to embarrass Watson in social situations. As the series progresses, and Lucy Liu's gift for playing the straight man becomes apparent, such scenes become more widespread, but the sole example in this episode comes when the detective joins her at the opera, but only in order to discuss the case and cause her to pretend not to see or hear him. It's worth noting that the short promos for each episode focus almost exclusively on the show's humorous elements.

My head is in a whirl: Watson thinks Holmes' act of auto-vandalism is part of a bigger plan, but if she's correct, we never find out what that plan is. It seems to be simply an act of sheer spite and rage.

It seems very likely that Mantlo could escape conviction for his wife's murder, given that the evidence proves only that he treated Saldua, a fact that would surely come under the category of doctor-patient confidentiality anyway.

"Consider every wretched hive of murder and depravity in this city my place of business." It's clear from the start that the team behind *Elementary* are playing a long game. Holmes and Watson are still quite cautious around one another, and their relationship throughout is notably frosty. Miller's performance suggests Nicol Williamson's twitchy, cocaine-addicted Holmes in the movie *The Seven-Per-Cent Solution*, struggling to overcome his cravings and prove his worth to the police.

1X02: While You Were Sleeping
US Airdate: 4 October 2012

Writer: Robert Doherty
Director: John David Coles

Guest Cast: Jennifer Ferrin (Rebecca Ellison); Bill Heck (Ty Morstan); Casey Siemaszko (Mike McGee); Rosa Arredondo (Elaine); Chris Bresky (Recovering Addict); Amy Landon (Yvette Ellison); Rey Lucas (Martin); Ken Marks (Moderator); Asa Somers (Doctor); Paul Michael Valley (Burley Man); Dj Nino Carta (Hospital Patient)*; Ava Paloma (Mary Margaret Phelps)*; Tom Stratford (Core Detective)*

*Uncredited

Plot: Casey McManus is shot in his home, having apparently surprised a burglar. Holmes deduces from the odour of deodorant that the killer was a woman. A witness provides the police with a description of the mysterious female, whom Detective Bell tracks down to St Isadora's hospital. But Yvette Ellison has been in a coma for three days and couldn't possibly have committed the crime, even though her deodorant matches that smelled by Holmes at the crime scene. He finds that Yvette has a twin, but Rebecca Ellison does not look at all like her sister.

There's a second shooting in Queens, and Holmes proves that the victim, Anna Webster, is related to Casey McManus. Anna was being watched by a private detective, Mike McGee, who reluctantly confesses that his clients were Yvette and Rebecca Ellison, who have been tracking down their late father's bastard children.

Rebecca admits to knowing that Casey and Anna could lay claim to some of the estate. Holmes is convinced that

Rebecca is the killer, but has no idea why she should have chosen to impersonate her comatose sister. Gregson is forced to release her when she provides an unbreakable alibi.

Confronting Rebecca at the hospital, Holmes informs her that there is another heir. Bell arrests Holmes after he makes a scene and punches the officer. But it's all a ruse, and Gregson arrests Yvette at the address of the third heir (who turns out to be an undercover police officer). Holmes and Watson explain to Rebecca that Yvette was having an affair with a doctor, who placed her in a medically-induced coma, from which she regularly emerged to commit the murders.

The best and the wisest man: Holmes has learned how to put himself into a trance during AA meetings. He doesn't share. He has a collection of locks, which he picks. He denies owning the violin Watson finds in the closet. When he is shown to be lying, he sets fire to it. At the end of the episode, he plays a (different?) pristine violin, though he is not seen to do so again for the remainder of the Season. He claims that half his face is leathery from the number of slaps he has received over the years. He has hacked Joan's e-mail.

I am lost without my Boswell: Watson displays her first glimmerings as a detective, pointing out something the cops missed. Holmes is impressed. Joan's parents have reached out to her ex-lover, Ty, regarding her (to them) inexplicable decision to switch careers. She hasn't been returning her mother's phone calls.

The efficiency of our detective police force: This episode marks the first appearance of Detective Bell, one of Gregson's "best guys." His first name, Marcus, is not revealed until late in the season, in the episode *Details*. He considers Holmes nuts and calls him "Harry Potter." Bell is presumably named for Dr Joseph Bell, Conan Doyle's original inspiration for Sherlock Holmes.

Gregson is happily married (and, we learn in *Dead Man's Switch*, a parent). He addresses Holmes as "Sherlock" here, but in later episodes switches to the more formal "Holmes." He found the consultant to be a pain when they met in London, and is apparently under the impression that Holmes was in London two weeks earlier rather than in rehab. Mike McGee is an old friend, and former colleague.

There is a strong family resemblance about misdeeds: Holmes explains his "attic theory" of how the mind works, taken directly from *A Study in Scarlet* (and also used in the *Sherlock* episode *The Great Game*). "It's important not to have useful facts... crowding out the useful ones." Without success, Watson points out to him that the brain doesn't work that way.

Holmes' skills as a violinist are mentioned throughout the Canon.

Ty bears the same surname – Morstan - as John H Watson's first wife Mary. It is never stated onscreen, however, and there is no suggestion that he might make a return appearance.

I have never loved: Holmes figures out that Ty is Watson's ex-lover, and advises her to sleep with him. She doesn't.

A seven-per-cent solution: The episode begins at an group support meeting. Holmes realises the solution at another meeting.

He recognises the signs of substance abuse in Gregson's

old friend Mike.

Watson promises to give Holmes a drug test when she returns from her dinner date.

He refuses Gregson's offer of a celebratory drink. This proves to have consequences in the episode *Rat Race*.

A certain unexpected vein of pawky humour: Watson's reaction when Holmes sets his violin alight is hilarious, particularly since, *Airplane*-style, we see him preparing the blaze in the background while she's on the phone. They argue over his plans to test whether or not Yvette is faking her coma by stabbing her in the thigh.

When Holmes mentions the familiar deodorant, Bell responds: "Too bad we can't put out an APB on an armpit."

Holmes, upon overhearing the name of Joan's ex: "Ty - funny name, that. Noun, verb, nationality."

My head is in a whirl: The episode title rather gives away the solution.

The pale stripe of skin left by a wedding ring on the doctor's finger is seen clearly in flashbacks, but is invisible in the original scene.

Holmes' ability to deduce Watson's recent lack of sexual activity based upon her gait is nonsense.

Is there no simpler way to trap Yvette than to stage such an elaborate charade? Wouldn't any of the hospital's security cameras show an apparently comatose patient walking around? Is this an example of Holmes' inability to resist a touch of the dramatic?

The CBS website lists Gregson's first name as Tobias, but here Mike McGee calls him "Tommy", not Toby. The *Elementary* writers' Twitter feed has confirmed that he is indeed called Thomas. Stranger still, a CBS interview with Aidan Quinn refers to his character as "Captain *Grayson*."

"Is it sad being wrong as often as you're right?"
The first really satisfying mystery of the series, with two highpoints – the first when Bell reveals that the prime suspect is in a coma, and the second when Holmes' theory that the murder was committed by Yvette Ellison's twin is shattered by the discovery that Rebecca is a fraternal rather than an identical twin sister. Lucy Liu is wasted in too many scenes where she is present but has not a single line of dialogue, as in the sequence at Mike McGee's office. This problem is addressed in later episodes.

1X03: Child Predator
US Airdate: 18 October 2012

Writer: Peter Blake
Director: Rod Holcomb

Guest Cast: Johnny Simmons (Adam Kemper); Yancey Arias (Robert Castillo); Michael Countryman (Barry Kemper); Erin Dilly (Amanda Kemper); Selenis Leyva (Sara Castillo); Christopher Evan Welch (Samuel Abbott); Larisa Polonsky (Lori Thomas); Flint Beverage (Sgt. O'Donnell); Andrew M Chamberlain (Adam Kemper Aged 12); Don Guillory (News Cameraman); Brian O'Neill (Kemper Family Attorney); José Báez (Prisoner); Katelynn Bailey (Mariana Castillo)*; Ludovic Coutaud (Prostitute)*

*Uncredited

Plot: Holmes is alerted via his police scanner to the abduction of Mariana Castillo, a 7-year old child. It's the work of a notorious criminal known as the Balloon Man (because of his habit of leaving a bunch of party balloons at the site of each crime).

Mr Castillo's ex-mistress was outside the family home on the night Mariana was taken, and she recalls seeing a dark brown van speeding past. Holmes and Watson find evidence that the vehicle may have been repainted. With this information, the police are able to track down the Balloon Man's decommissioned NYPD van. But the driver is too young to be the kidnapper. Holmes recognises him as Adam Kemper, the Balloon Man's first victim, taken at age 12 in 2005.

The youth is far from forthcoming, but after speaking to him, Holmes realises that the Balloon Man has a night job delivering newspapers. From this deduction, the police are able to identify the kidnapper as Samuel Abbott, but when they storm his last known address, they find only a memory stick on which Abbott has recorded a demand for Adam's return, in exchange for Mariana.

Adam accepts immunity and gives up the location of Abbott's hideout. The police rescue the girl, but Abbott shoots himself rather than be captured. An examination of the apartment brings Holmes to a horrifying conclusion: Abbott isn't the Balloon Man, Adam is! He's dominated Abbott ever since he was snatched and from the age of 14 ordered the adult to commit further abductions.

The immunity agreement means that he can't be charged for any crimes committed in concert with Abbott. But his abductor was in hospital during the killing of the fifth victim, William Crawford, in 2009. Adam therefore acted alone, and can be arrested for murder.

The best and the wisest man: Holmes lies to Watson about his intention to join her on a jog. He first became interested in the Balloon Man while still in London. He prefers to talk rather than to listen, once to a phrenology bust he named Angus (shades of the skull the BBC's Sherlock deems a friend.) He was sent to boarding school at age 5. He tells Adam Kemper that he was bullied there by a boy named Anders Larson (the name has no Canonical associations whatsoever). He later indicates that the story may not have been entirely true. He doesn't sleep during a case. He mans his scanner again in *Flight Risk*.

I am lost without my Boswell: Watson, too, remembers the Balloon Man's crimes. She exercised to keep herself awake while cramming for tests at medical school, where she was valedictorian. At the end of the episode, she brews a cup of tea intended to detoxify and cleanse Holmes' system.

The efficiency of our detective police force: This is the first episode in which Gregson and Holmes are seen to be at odds, after the consultant asks to interview Adam Kemper. He's threatened by the Castillo family when he refuses to hand Adam over to Abbott.

Bell is in the episode, too, but his involvement is minimal to say the least. Get used to this - Jon Michael Hill is criminally underused in many episodes.

There is a strong family resemblance about misdeeds: Holmes quotes a famous line from Conan Doyle's first novel, *A Study in Scarlet*: "From a drop of water, a logician can infer the possibility of an Atlantic or a Niagara without having seen or heard of either one."

I have never loved: Holmes lists prostitutes as being among those to whom he enjoyed talking about his cases while living in London.

A seven-per-cent solution: Watson is shocked when she spots Holmes handling a bottle of wine in the Castillo's fridge. This is a surprisingly drug-free episode, considering how early on it is in the Holmes-Watson relationship.

A certain unexpected vein of pawky humour: The scene where Watson teaches Holmes to stay awake by performing squats is the first suggestion of a bond between the two beside the purely professional. The fact that Holmes is prepared to look silly by taking her advice may not be hilarious, but it's oddly sweet.

He admits to lying when he agreed to join Watson on a jog. "When I say I agree with you, it means I'm not listening." he reinforces the point, by agreeing with her moments later.

My head is in a whirl: Why on earth do the cops who enter Samuel Abbott's home handle the memory stick with their bare hands?

"I handed a psychopath a Get Out of Jail Free card."
The previous episode may have offered several surprising twists, but the revelation of Adam's guilt is more satisfying still, aided in no small part by Johnny Simmons' unsettling performance. It's a real shame that Peter Blake has only written one more episodes for the series, *You Do it to Yourself*.

1X04: The Rat Race
US Airdate: 25 October 2012

Writer: Craig Sweeny
Director: Rosemary Rodriguez

Guest Cast: Craig Bierko (Jim Fowkes); Molly Price (Donna Kaplan); Luke Kirby (Aaron Ward); Jennifer Van Dyck (Alyssa Talbott); Andrew Pang (Dan Cho); Susan Pourfar (Emily Hankins); Tim Ewing (Sommelier); Judy Kuhn (Board Member); Nicole Patrick (Barista); Stephen Plunkett (Martin Rydell); Alison Walla (Girlfriend); Lim Ferguson (Local Sheriff)*

*Uncredited

Plot: Holmes and Watson are summoned by the board of directors of investment firm Canon-Ebersole. Their COO Peter Talbot has vanished, and an examination of his office reveals that the executive has a fondness for prostitutes.

The search ends at an apartment in Tribeca, but when Holmes and Watson find Talbot, he is dead, apparently from a heroin overdose. The NYPD consider his death accidental, but Holmes is intrigued by the fact that Talbot's predecessor died from peanut allergies, another convenient accident. He begins to suspect that several Canon-Ebersole executives may have been murdered by an ambitious colleague.

In a stroke of inspiration, he realises that the killer is not prime suspect Jim Fowkes, but his secretary, Donna Kaplan. She has killed in order to ensure Fowkes' rise to power (and, by extension, hers). Confronting her, Holmes is zapped by Donna's taser. She intends to bury him on Fowkes' property.

In an attempt to put Watson off the scent, Donna replies to one of her texts, omitting Holmes' preferred use of abbreviations. When Joan realises he couldn't have sent the message, she alerts Gregson, and the cops arrive just as Donna is forcing Holmes to dig his own grave.

The best and the wisest man: Holmes loves text-speak, and Watson considers his abbreviations indecipherable, a fact that saves his life at the episode's climax. Gregson calls him a weirdo (though he also apparently tells Jim Fowkes that Holmes is the finest investigator he's ever known). He loathes bankers and considers them crooks. He has no rate of pay. He thinks most of the killers he's known rather dreary. He is not a fan of John Maynard Keynes. He can imitate an American accent pretty well and speaks Mandarin, though not as well as he'd like. This is the first time we see Holmes attempt to solve a case by pinning up all available documented evidence above the fireplace in the brownstone. For the first but not the last time this season, Holmes gets out of a pair of handcuffs.

I am lost without my Boswell: The opening scene of the episode shows Watson breaking client-patient confidentiality in order to locate Holmes. She too speaks Mandarin, but not as well as her mother would like. She's never been married, so we know that her former partner, Ty (seen in *While You Were Sleeping*), is not an ex-husband.

The efficiency of our detective police force: Gregson is again at odds with Holmes when the consultant asks to interrogate Peter Talbot's widow. When Holmes finally confesses his addiction problems, the policeman tells him that he already knew, having tested him with the offer of a drink during *While You Were Sleeping*.

Bell, who, again, barely appears, is similarly unimpressed with Holmes' suggestion that someone may have laced Talbot's salad with heroin.

There is a strong family resemblance about misdeeds: There are no Canonical quotes or references in this episode. Shame.

I have never loved: Watson suggests that Holmes may be as familiar with prostitutes as Peter Talbot.

Her friend sets her up with a blind date, Aaron Ward. She puts her hair up whenever she meets an attractive man. Joan suspects Aaron is married, and Holmes confirms her suspicions. Aaron insists he married a woman from Kosovo to get her citizenship. Unnerved by the fact that she spotted his lie, he breaks up with her.

A seven-per-cent solution: Watson is dismayed when Holmes orders the most expensive bottle of wine on a restaurant menu, charging it to his employers. He sends it over to a courting couple.

The presence of heroin in the room where Peter Talbot died causes Joan to worry that Sherlock might relapse at any moment. Holmes is familiar with the typical apartment of a heroin addict and with the smell of cooked heroin. Watson administers a drug test to Holmes after her date.

A certain unexpected vein of pawky humour: After his investigation stalls, Holmes slams a basketball into the floor repeatedly, claiming it helps him think, but in reality he's probably doing it to get rid of Watson.

Prime suspect Jim Fowkes: "Do you know what it takes just to survive at a place like Canon-Ebersole?" Holmes: "I'd think avoiding you would be a good start."

My head is in a whirl: Why didn't Donna Kaplan remove the salad containing heroin from Talbot's secret apartment? Without it, Holmes would have no reason to suspect murder. Having been so careful in all her previous murders, this seems like a careless but very convenient lapse.

Gregson claims that he tested Holmes by offering to buy him a drink some weeks earlier, but in the pilot, the two of them are seen together in an Irish pub.

"If I'm going to get in bed with the croupiers of a rigged game, I'm going to make damn sure their wallets are lighter in the morning." A solid episode, utilising what will become a standard *Elementary* plot device, a previously unsuspected second mystery arising from the resolution of the first. For the second time since the pilot, Holmes almost fails to give Watson the credit she deserves. It's pleasant to see him suitably humbled in the closing scenes, but of course, there's no way it'll last.

1X05: Lesser Evils
US Airdate:1 November 2012

Writer: Liz Friedman
Director: Colin Bucksey

Guest Cast: David Harbour (Dr Mason Baldwin); David Constabile (Danilo Gura); Ben Rappaport (Dr Cahill); Jenni Barber (Jacqueline Zoltana); Anika Noni Rose (Dr Carrie Dwyer); Eric Deskin (Richard Sanchez); Jonathan C Kaplan (Barista Dave); Jay Klaitz (Bruce); Shauna Miles (Nurse); Eric Engleman (Security Guard); Rozi Baker (Morgan Duncan); Mike Getz (Trent Kelty)*; Shawn Gonzalez (Reporter)*

*Uncredited

Plot: Visiting Chandler Memorial hospital, Holmes spots the body of Trent Kelty in the mortuary, and instantly believes that the old man was murdered, the crime disguised as a heart attack.

He finds evidence that someone in the dead man's room had purchased a drink from a nearby coffee shop. A chat with a horny barista leads Holmes and Watson to Kelty's female visitor. She tells them that the old man, who was dying of cancer, often had late-night discussions with a doctor regarding pain relief. Holmes believes that the hospital has its own Angel of Death, who has taken the lives of at least nine terminal patients.

Prime suspect is Dr Mason Baldwin, a surgeon who specialises in high-risk cases. Holmes and Watson capture a Dr Cahill as he is in the process of stealing morphine from his patients. Under interrogation, Cahill claims to have heard one of the Angel's victims conversing with the mysterious doctor about his condition.

Watson discovers that one of the Angel's victims, Samantha Cropsy, rather than being a hopeless case, was in fact recovering from her illness.

Realizing that the killer conversed with one of his victims in Ukranian, Holmes identifies the Angel as Danilo Gura, the hospital's janitor and a former doctor in his home country. Gura confesses to all the killings but insists that Samantha Cropsy was, according to her chart, a hopeless case. The chart was altered by Dr Baldwin, who knew about Gura's activities. Bates made an error when operating on Samantha, and, fearing his career would be in jeopardy if his mistake became known, set about turning Samantha into the ideal victim for the Angel of Death.

The best and the wisest man: Holmes has Watson buy him tickets to the Arms and Armour exhibit at the Met. Presumably, once he becomes involved with Kelty's death he doesn't have time to attend. He modestly considers himself a wise man. When Watson suggests sushi for dinner, he lists all the various conditions one can suffer from following the consumption of raw fish.

I am lost without my Boswell: Joan lost touch with her old friend, Dr Carrie Dwyer, and other former colleagues after the death of her patient. As a result, she is uncomfortable in a hospital environment. She correctly diagnoses the heart attack suffered by the first victim. She let her licence expire, but led Holmes to believe she was no longer permitted to practice medicine. She's the one who figures out that Kelty's blonde visitor is not a doctor but a beautician. A subplot involves Joan diagnosing a 12 year-old girl's heart condition against all available evidence. Watson apparently requests the appropriate tests for the child, despite having no authority to do so. At the end of the episode, she deletes all the photos on her laptop of her time as a doctor.

The efficiency of our detective police force: Yet again aggravated by Holmes' actions, Gregson insists that Holmes apologise to the hospital's administrator Sanchez.

Bell's skilled interrogation of Dr Cahill is ruined by Holmes, who doesn't believe him guilty of murder.

There is a strong family resemblance about misdeeds: As described by Stamford in *A Study in Scarlet*, Holmes is seen strangling a body in the morgue in order to determine post-mortem bruising. OK, he beat the corpses in *A Study in Scarlet*, but there was probably a little strangling going on, too.

Holmes' love of bees is mentioned again: he and the morgue attendant Bruce frequent the same beekeeping forum.

I have never loved: Holmes has his fingers crossed that Joan and Carrie fell out over a failed sapphic dalliance.

A seven-per-cent solution: Holmes is annoyed at himself for failing to identify Dr Cahill as a former addict.

A certain unexpected vein of pawky humour: Holmes callously throws liquid into the corridor to ensure that Gura the cleaner stops work in Kelty's room. Gura gets his own back by pressing multiple buttons in the hospital lift in order to inconvenience Holmes.

Mocking Sanchez for his shortness, Holmes asks Baldwin, "Do you reach things off high shelves for this one?"

Joan explains away Holmes' tactlessness by claiming that he has a form of Tourette's.

My head is in a whirl: Although Holmes compliments Gura's accent, it's hard to believe that Cahill didn't realise that the voice he overheard wasn't that of an American.

Again, the flashbacks cheat. The fabric wrapped round Gura's trolley (which Holmes deduces match the colours of the Ukranian flag) aren't visible in the original scene.

"So you're too indifferent to your patients to be the Angel of Death? That's a novel alibi." The plot rehashes the major gimmick from the pilot: the villain turning his target into the ideal victim for a killer. Once again, the apparent resolution of the Angel of Death case throws up another puzzle. But the writing is good, and the setting novel, so the episode gets away with it. Even Joan's largely irrelevant subplot doesn't stick around long enough to tax the viewer's patience. Even though this is a very Watson-heavy episode, Miller acquits himself well.

1X06: Flight Risk
US Airdate: 8 November 2012

Writer: Corrine Brinkerhoff
Director: David Platt

Guest Cast: Reiko Aylesworth (Miranda Molinari); Brian Kerwin (Charles Cooper); Roger Rees (Allistair); Adam LeFevre (Ed Hairston); Matthew Humphreys (Owen Bates); Ashley Bryant (Hostess); Michelle Federer (Ellie Wilson); James Michael Reilly (Walter Devlin); David Shumbris (Hank Gerard)*

*****Uncredited**

Plot: After a slow week, Holmes is excited at the news that a small plane has crashed on Far Rockaway Beach. There are no survivors. The three passengers were attorneys, but only two died as a result of the crash. Holmes finds that one of them, Hank Gerard, was murdered.

Charles Cooper, the head of Key Star Charters insists that Joe Newell, the pilot on the doomed flight was incapable of any irresponsible act that might have led to the crash.

Bell reports that the law firm to which the three attorneys belonged was engaged in a class action case against a food company with regard to their allegedly carcinogenic sugar substitute.

Gerard's role at the firm was in jeopardy, and it seems likely that he attacked his boss, Walter Devlin, during the flight. The plane's black box recording appears to confirm this – Devlin can apparently be heard arguing with Gerard. But Holmes deduces that Devlin was leaving a message on Gerard's cell phone, not realising that his employee was already dead, his body stowed in the cargo hold of the plane.

Charles Cooper produces security camera footage of Gerard arguing with Ed Hairston, employee of the food company involved in the legal action. Hairston admits to being the whistle blower who supplied Gerard with information. They argued because he refused to testify, but his physical disability means that he was incapable of killing Gerard.

Holmes proves that the plane's fuel tank was filled with sand – the flight was doomed to crash, and Gerard was killed when he confronted the saboteur.

One of Key Star's other pilots, Owen Barts, has been smuggling drugs from Florida. Holmes thinks Barts sabotaged the flight to prevent the pilot, Newell, from alerting the authorities. Barts insists that Cooper will alibi him, but the next morning, Cooper informs the police that Barts confessed to him over the phone.

Barts has vanished, and the weapon used to kill Gerard is found in his garage. But Holmes suspects that Barts, too, has been killed by an accomplice – Charles Cooper. The smell of model glue fumes suggests to Holmes that Barts cut Cooper during their struggle, and Cooper used superglue to seal up the wound.

The best and the wisest man: Holmes knows all the police emergency codes, and considers himself an expert on aviation disasters. Watson gradually realises the reason for this fascination: he's afraid of flying. He insists he's not phobic, but his anxiety is the result of his observational prowess. Joan thinks Sherlock is taking an interest in the case purely in order to avoid seeing his father, who is apparently coming to New York to check on his son's progress. In fact, Sherlock knows that the man he calls "a serial absentee" has no intention of showing up. He's right, and to prove it, has an old friend named Allistair take his father's place. Allistair is a former actor who coached Sherlock on his accents. Holmes broke his wrist during childhood, then set the bone himself. Eventually, he got a tattoo to cover the scar. He uses a magnifying lens app on his mobile phone. His manner of speech is becoming ever more archaic, making pop culture references to Charlie Brown seem very peculiar indeed.

I am lost without my Boswell: Joan has no doubt that Holmes' father will meet her to discuss her son's case. Understandably, she's thoroughly unamused by his rather heartless practical joke. She deduces that Allistair works in a bookshop from a brief glance at the receipt that falls from his book. Zadie Smith is one of her favourite authors.

The efficiency of our detective police force: Gregson promises to send Holmes some cold case documents to keep him busy.

Bell actually seems to spend more time working with Holmes on the case than Watson does.

There is a strong family resemblance about misdeeds: Roger Rees, who plays Sherlock's friend Allistair, was a memorable Holmes in the 1988 BBC Radio adaptation of *The Hound of the Baskervilles*. His character even makes passing reference to acting in British radio dramas – shame we haven't seen Allistair in the series since this episode.

The second pilot at Key Star Charters is apparently named Barts (see **My head is in a whirl**), perhaps in reference to the London Hospital where Holmes and Watson met in *A Study in Scarlet*.

The clue about the strong odour of glue, first in Cooper's office, and then on the man himself, suggests – probably unintentionally - one of the later stories, *The Retired Colourman*.

I have never loved: Joan is stunned when Allistair, in the role of Holmes' father, asks her about the quality of the sex with his son.

A seven-per-cent solution: Holmes tries very hard not to inhale the model glue fumes in Charles Cooper's office.
   Allistair tells Joan he thought Holmes was simply dabbling, until he appeared at the actor's door nine months ago, unable to speak. During his fits, he muttered the name "Irene" repeatedly.

A certain unexpected vein of pawky humour: The scene where Joan is humiliated in the restaurant by the ersatz Holmes Sr is too mean to be funny, but her shock at waking to find Holmes at the foot of her bed, ready to admit the truth about his fear of flying raises a smile.

My head is in a whirl: Holmes says that his father secured Joan's services as a sober companion via e-mail, but we discover in *Deja Vu All Over Again* that it was actually Sherlock himself who selected her, and that she is well aware of the fact.
   It's quite a stretch that even Holmes is able to notice the difference between particular grains of sand on a beach. It's fortunate that he does, of course, since it has an important bearing on the plot.
   According the the credits, the drug smuggling pilot is named Owen Bates, but everyone pronounces his surname "Barts."

"You can't expect Sherlock Holmes to relate to you the way others might. The moment you do, he'll migrate

out of your life, and you'll be the poorer for it." A brilliantly complex episode, piling revelation upon revelation, this is easily one of *Elementary*'s top five episodes. By this time, the makers have fixed it so that Joan doesn't appear in every scene with Sherlock, regardless of whether or not she has anything to contribute. She's conspicuously absent from several interrogations in this episode. The episode ends with Joan asking Holmes about Irene, a moment that will have massive implications.

1X07: One Way to Get Off
US Airdate: 15 November 2012

Writer: Christopher Silber
Director: Seith Mann

Guest Cast: Callie Thorne (Terry D'Amico); Keith Szarabajka (Wade Crewes); Stephen Kunken (Dr Carrow); Stephen McKinley Henderson (Groundskeeper Edison); Brian Tarantina (Walsh); Amy Hohn (Dr Ryan); Stivi Paskoski (Victor Nardin); Steven Skybell (Dr Sacco); Juan Castano (Sean Figueroa); Evgeniya Petkova Radilova (Katya); Cheryl Lewis (Allison Willis)*; Gilbert Soto (Bookstore Patron)*; Greg Wattkis (Mike Willis)*

*Uncredited

Plot: A particularly violent crime scene bears an uncanny similarity to a series of murders committed by Wade Crewes in 1999. Gregson considers the robbery-homicide either the work of a copycat or a bizarre coincidence. But Holmes believes that Crewes may have had an accomplice, who is now continuing his crime spree.

The most recent victims received threatening e-mails from contractor Julian Walsh. When questioned, Walsh is certainly anxious, but Holmes discovers that his anxiety is because he is keeping a woman prisoner in his basement. Not only has he an alibi in his sex slave, but a ballistics comparison shows that the gun used in the original Wade Crewes murders also killed the two most recent victims.

Holmes invites Gregson's former partner Terry D'Amico to participate in the present investigation. From his cell at Sing Sing, Crewes protests his innocence, accusing Gregson of planting his fingerprints on a mug found at one of the crime scenes. He insists that he was with a married woman, Carla Figueroa, at the time of the murders, but she refused to testify. When Holmes and Gregson call at her house, Carla's son Sean informs them that she is dead.

Viewing the interrogation tapes, Holmes sees Gregson hand Crewes the mug that was later used to incriminate him. Gregson knows that the mug was planted by his former partner, Terry.

Victor Nardan, an early suspect in the home invasion killings, is missing, but Holmes and Watson track him down to a hotel in Brighton Beach. Nardan isn't around, but the murder weapon is found hidden under a loose floorboard in his room. After another murder, Holmes is satisfied that Nardan is innocent – he is blind in his right eye, and couldn't possibly have shot anyone.

It seems that Crewes is supplying someone on the outside with information about his crimes. Holmes finds that one of the volunteers at Sing Sing library was Sean Figueroa, the son of Carla Figueroa and Wade Crewes. Sean committed the murders in order to establish his father's innocence.

The best and the wisest man: After Watson's enquiry regarding Irene in the previous episode, Holmes has decided to respond to her remarks tersely without engaging in conversation. He ditches her in the opening scene in order to respond to Gregson's request for assistance. The ringer on his cell phone is the music from *Psycho*. He's read *War and Peace* and recognises an Oscar Wilde quote. He uses his faultless American accent once again. He eventually tells Watson that Irene is dead.

I am lost without my Boswell: Watson considers it her job to overstep polite boundaries. Having run out of options now that her charge has become uncooperative, she's forced to visit Hemdale Rehabilitation Facility in an attempt to dig up further information. Holmes asks for her assistance when he suspects Wade Crewes may have been framed, because he considers her good at dealing with the "moral component."

The efficiency of our detective police force: For Captain Gregson, the arrest of Crewes was "a career-defining case." His partner at that time was Terry D'Amico. For once, he is reluctant to consider Holmes' theories, and simmers with rage throughout the episode, particularly when Holmes tells him about the planted mug. Confronting D'Amico, Gregson tells her he is prepared to see his career come to an end should turn out that an innocent man has gone to prison.

Bell briefs the task force on the murder investigation, and interrogates Victor Nardan. This is really Gregson's episode, though, and the young policeman has only a small part to play.

There is a strong family resemblance about misdeeds: The story *The Norwood Builder* concerns the planting of an incriminating fingerprint. In that case, however, the accused man was innocent; despite the fact that the evidence against him is a forgery, Crewes is actually guilty.

Though Irene's surname is not stated, it can be seen on the envelopes: Adler.

The writers seem to have given up on including Canonical quotations in the dialogue.

I have never loved: Holmes tells Joan that his bodily fluids are at her disposal. He's actually talking about his saliva (see **A seven-per-cent solution**).

He never mentioned Irene during his therapy sessions at

Hemdale. Joan is given several letters from Irene which Holmes left with the groundskeeper, Edison (they became friends over a shared love of bees). Joan gives them back to Holmes without reading them, whereupon he puts them in the blender (shades of his violin-burning in *While You Were Sleeping*).

A seven-per-cent solution: An abrupt Holmes informs Watson that he is willing to undergo drug testing every two hours.

A certain unexpected vein of pawky humour: When receiving a call from Watson, Holmes pretends that the signal is weak, not realising that she is stood right behind him. Busted.
  Joan, upon seeing Victor's hotel: "He's not here. If I lived here, I wouldn't be here either."
  Holmes: "I left some urine in your room." Watson: "Tell me it's in a cup."

My head is in a whirl: In the opening scene, Holmes' phone sounds when he receives a text from Gregson. It's a generic alarm sound. After the opening titles, the phone plays the music from *Psycho*'s classic shower scene. Did he change it in honour of the case? If so, it's a rather ghoulish thing to do, even by Holmes' standards.

"Always nice when a psychopath grooms himself to look the part, don't you think?" The opening sequence of this episode, with a masked intruder executing two victims with pillows strapped to their heads is positively macabre, and the cut to Joan preparing a reddish drink in a blender suggests a Hitchcokian influence (reinforced by the use of the music from *Psycho*). But the plot soon becomes a rather generic police procedural, with the deductions regarding Victor Nardan's vision the only remotely Holmesian element. Holmes and Watson have gone from being inseparable to barely spending any screen time together in the first half of the show. There has to be a happy medium.

1X08: The Long Fuse
US Airdate: 29 November 2012

Writer: Jeffrey Paul King
Director: Andrew Bernstein

Guest Cast: Lisa Edelstein (Heather Vanowen); John Pankow (Edgar Knowles); Donnie Keshawarz (Earl Wheeler); Adam Mucci (Rennie James); Deepa Purohit (Himali Singh); Rufus Collins (Adrian); Dan Bittner (David Preston); Charles Socarides (Royce Maltz); Vedant Gokhale (Pradeep Singh); Steve Cirbus (Bomb Squad Tech); Caris Vujcec (Recovering Addict); Tom Titone (Lobbyist)

Plot: An explosion at the offices of Parabolic Web Industries kills two employees and injures many more. Holmes believes that the bomb was detonated remotely – a pager is found to be one of the weapon's components.

Plumber Renny Jacobs is questioned by the NYPD, but it seems he was trying to contact his favourite deli – a simple wrong number set off the bomb.

An examination of the newspaper packed into the bomb shows that the device was planted four years earlier, at which time the wrecked offices were occupied by Vanowen Strategic Communications. Four years ago, however, the pager connected to the bomb was out of range of any signal towers, and couldn't have been activated.

Heather Vanowen tells Holmes and Watson that she has received threatening letters from eco-terrorist group the Earth Liberty Organization. An oft-repeated phrase in those letters leads Holmes to Edgar Knowles, who reluctantly confesses to planting several bombs, but insists he did not attack Vanowen SC.

Holmes is interested by the speedy rise within Heather's company of Pradeep Singh, who disappeared after a disagreement with his superior, Wheeler. At the Singh family home, Pradeep's wife tells Holmes and Watson she's certain he was murdered. Examining the living room in her absence, Holmes finds that Pradeep's corpse has been hidden behind a wall for the last four years. Mrs Singh is in the clear, however, having been in Mumbai at the time of her husband's disappearance. Holmes deduces that the bomb was meant for Singh.

A key found on the body leads to a videotape stored in a safety deposit box. The tape shows a young Pradeep Singh with a prostitute – Heather Vanowen. When Singh realised that his boss was a former hooker, he began to blackmail her. After her first attempt to kill her tormentor with a bomb failed, Heather simply shot Pradeep and walled him up.

The best and the wisest man: In addition to the multiple television memory test, Holmes is simultaneously reading a book. He reminds Watson how much he dislikes bankers, a reference to *Rat Race*. This is the second time in two episodes that Holmes uses the excuse of using a suspect's toilet to search their home; last week it was Julian Walsh, here it's Pradeep Singh's wife – he does the same thing again in *Details*. He enjoys watching '70s and '80s police interrogations, when techniques were rawer.

I am lost without my Boswell: Watson tells Holmes she doesn't have another client lined up. She thinks Holmes will miss her when she's gone, an assertion he disputes.

The efficiency of our detective police force: Gregson seems a little ticked off when Holmes informs him that though Edgar Knowles is guilty of several bombings, he is innocent of the Vanowen SC incident. As a result, he's not his usually cooperative self.

Bell has never been to Holmes' residence (He's first seen there in *The Deductionist*). He didn't enjoy the 1980 comedy *Cheech and Chong's Next Movie*, over a copy of which Pradeep Singh has recorded his liaison with prostitute Heather Vanowen.

There is a strong family resemblance about misdeeds: The crossword clue element of the plot seems better suited to an Inspector Morse novel than a Sherlock Holmes adventure.

Blackmail victims who resort to murder turn up several times in the canon, most notably in *The Boscombe Valley Mystery*. Holmes is usually more sympathetic with them than he is with Heather. Is it because two innocent employees of Parabolic Web Industries are killed by her bomb?

In *The Dancing Men*, Holmes experiments with malodorous chemicals. Here, he constructs miniature fertilizer bombs, but is at least gracious enough to do so on the roof of the brownstone rather than indoors. The Canonical Holmes was never so considerate.

I have never loved: Heather Vanowen is clearly attracted to Holmes. They share a love of crosswords. He tells her he's too busy for sex, but suggests fixing an appointment for a later date.

Holmes instantly identifies the woman in the video as a high-end prostitute. He considers the anti-prostitution laws in the US "Victorian."

A seven-per-cent solution: Watson, knowing that her time as sober companion will be up in a few weeks, urges Holmes to find a sponsor. She introduces him to Adrian, whom he dismisses within moments. Instead, he picks former car thief Alfredo Llamosa, whom he nevertheless avoids when Watson sets up a meeting. Alfredo will appear in several future episodes, acting both as Holmes' sponsor and as a member of his New York Irregulars.

Holmes examines the letters from the ELM at an AA meeting.

Heather accuses Holmes of being a fellow addict – she's talking about crosswords.

A certain unexpected vein of pawky humour: Heather's offence at Holmes' reaction to her seduction attempts is the only really amusing moment in a pretty straight-faced episode.

My head is in a whirl: Holmes says of the wrecked Parabolic Web Industries offices, "pre-explosion, this place looked like the deck of a starship." How does he know?

Another act of carelessness traps a killer: if only Heather had removed the safety deposit box key from Pradeep Singh's key chain when she hid the body. Why on Earth did she go to the trouble of moving her entire business to another office building after killing Singh? Why not just remove the bomb?

"I'm entirely self-sufficient." Apart from introducing the audience to semi-regular character Alfredo, this is a pretty workmanlike segment. The discovery of Singh's body is nicely handled, but Heather is the only serious suspect, and her guilt is established well before the climax.

1X09: You Do It To Yourself
US Airdate: 6 December 2012

Writer: Peter Blake
Director: Phil Abraham

Guest Cast: Adam Rothenberg (Liam Danow); Kristy Wu (Jun Annunzio); Cameron Scoggins (Brendan O'Brien); Lord Jamar (Raul Ramirez); Richard Topol (Trent Annunzio); Randall Duk Kim (Old Man); Kevin Henderson (ND Detective); Andy Royce (Young Boy)

Plot: Bell invites Holmes and Watson to examine a corpse discovered in an abandoned building. Despite his fever, Holmes has no difficulty in identifying the dead man, who has been shot in both eyes, as Trent Annunzio, Professor at Garrison University.

Annunzio's wife Jun, a former student from Beijing, claims that Trent told her he would be attending a department meeting on the night of his death, but his teaching assistant, Brendan O'Brien, knows of no such meeting.

Holmes deduces that Annunzio spent the evening at a Chinese gambling parlour. At one such club he finds traces of a shooting. Things really seem to be going the detective's way when the proprietor – who had the body dumped far away from his establishment – reluctantly hands over security camera footage of the killing of Trent Annunzio.

Bell identifies the shooter as Raul Ramirez, who claims that he was hired to kill Annunzio by someone he only ever spoke to on the telephone. The caller specified that the victim must be shot in both eyes.

The cellphone on which the killing was arranged is discovered in Brendan O'Brien's apartment. To Holmes' disbelief, the young man confesses, but upon realising that O'Brien was having an affair with Annunzio's wife, he suspects Jun may have killed her husband and framed her own lover. Jun tells the police that Annunzio tortured her and, because the two were never actually married, held the threat of deportation over her head.

Holmes learns that Annunzio was self-medicating for eye pain – he had untreatable cancer. The mysterious individual who arranged Annunzio's death was Annunzio himself, wishing to frame Jun's lover and destroy all traces of his untreatable illness. Gregson is unconvinced by the scenario, but Joan points Holmes in the right direction: before settling on Ramirez, Annunzio first approached sex offender Dennis Kominski. Video footage shows Annunzio leaving Kominski a payoff. O'Brien is released, and he and Jun are married.

The best and the wisest man: Holmes subscribes to several personal security journals. He's fighting a fever throughout the episode, and blames that for his failure to note an important clue about a photo of Trent Annunzio. He's not a fan of Celine Dion. He feels guilty that he has put Mrs Annunzio in a position where she will likely be deported. For this episode only, he's taken to studying the evidence in the bathroom.

I am lost without my Boswell: Joan is contacted by Liam Danow, a former lover who has been arrested on a hit-and-run charge. She tells Holmes that Liam was a former client, but that proves to be a lie; they met when she was still working in the ER and became a couple thereafter. After proving Liam innocent, she arranges treatment for him. By the end of the episode, he hasn't shown up at the clinic. She has a good friend at the DA's office (strange that fact has never come up in any of the cases she's handled with Holmes thus far, nor will it for the remainder of the season). Using herbs purchased in Chinatown, she treats Holmes with a blend of tea her mother used to prepare for her (the same one she brews in *Child Predator?*). Holmes initially refuses to acknowledge its efficacy, but later requests more.

The efficiency of our detective police force: Bell used to work on the vice squad. When beating Holmes to a deduction, he wants the detective to ask him how he knew; Holmes remains tight-lipped. Like the same writer's *Flight Risk*, Bell and Holmes spend more time working on the case than Holmes and Watson.

Gregson appears in only three scenes in this episode. Amazingly, he doesn't have Brendan O'Brien charged with wasting police time. What a softie.

There is a strong family resemblance about misdeeds: The Canonical Holmes loves penning monographs on the subject of detection. They are mentioned in many stories, including *The Sign of Four*, *The Boscombe Valley Mystery*, *A Case of Identity*, *The Dancing Men* and *The Abbey Grange*. Here, he's considering writing a monograph on the effect of the tide levels upon crime rates in New York.

I have never loved: Joan tells Holmes that the tea prepared by her mother has been scientifically proven to result in longer-lasting erections. "By your mother?" he asks.

He deduces that Liam and Joan were lovers, but insists he doesn't judge her for it.

A seven-per-cent solution: Unlike Holmes, Liam has gone back to using drugs, and was too far gone on the night of the hit-and-run to recall whether he was driving or not. Holmes calls him "my brother in trackmarked arms."

A certain unexpected vein of pawky humour: The tea sequence is typical of the byplay we will see much more of as the relationship between Holmes and Watson gradually becomes less combative.
  Bell: "Tell me something I don't know." Holmes: "A pig's orgasm lasts up to thirty minutes."

My head is in a whirl: Watson's position as Holmes' sober companion is, according to *Rat Race*, supposed to be a secret between the two of them and Gregson, but at the crime scene, she talks about Holmes' father employing her within earshot of Detective Bell.

"Not everyone's a criminal mastermind." Holmes' identification of the body is a delight, pure canon. The idea of someone arranging their own murder in order to frame a faithless lover is by no means a new one, certainly nowhere near as surprising as the revelation in Blake's previous episode. At this point, the series seems to be running on the spot. The episode title, by the way, appears to have been appropriated from the subtitle of the very splendid song *Just* by Radiohead, memorably covered by Mark Ronson. Pity that, like the title of *While You Were Sleeping*, it rather gives the game away regarding the solution.

1X10: The Leviathan
US Airdate: 13 December 2012

Writers: Corrine Brinkerhoff & Craig Sweeny
Director: Peter Werner

Guest Cast: Freda Foh Shen (Mary Watson); Gbenga Akkinagbe (Jeremy Lopez); Reg Rogers (Micah Erlich); Sean Dugan (Charles Briggs); John Bolger (David Batonvert); Tonya Glanz (Gwen/Olivia Lynch); Dee Hoty (Patsy); Glenn Kalison (Alan Kent); Jennifer Kim (Gabrielle Harper); Nathaniel McIntyre (Uniform); Sue Simmons (Reporter); Alice Niedermair-Ludwig (Physical Therapist); Rosemary Howard (Amelie Widomski); Steve Garfanti (K9 Police Officer)*

*Uncredited

Plot: Micah Erlich, head engineer of Casterly Rock Security is concerned about his company's reputation after their "impregnable" vault the Leviathan has been cracked... twice. The four criminals who committed the original robbery have all been jailed. Erlich hires Holmes to find out how the most recent crime, in which $40m in diamonds were taken, was committed.

Charles Briggs, one of the original team of robbers agrees to talk to Holmes and Watson. He tells them that, before his death in prison, the actual safecracker Carter Averill was contacted by a legendary thief known as Le Chevalier.

Holmes takes no time at all in identifying philanthropist Peter Kent as Le Chevalier. He's quite correct, and is even able to recover a stolen Van Gogh from Kent's home, but Kent's son informs them that his father suffered a serious stroke two years earlier. He is in no state to have broken into the Leviathan.

A chance remark by Watson causes Holmes to suspect that someone at Carter Averill's trial may have deduced precisely how the heist was pulled off. A scrawled coffee order used as evidence against the conspirators holds the answer – Averill used an obscure programming language, which is printed on the other side of the order, to attack the Leviathan's random number generator.

Holmes supposes that one of the jurors, Justin Guthrie, a former software engineer, must have cracked the code, but by the time they reach his apartment, Guthrie is dead. His murder has been disguised as a suicide, but traces of his killer's blood are discovered. Checking the dead man's phone, Holmes finds the names of three other jurors. Together, all four may have possessed the skills necessary to steal the diamonds. Another of Holmes' suspects, Alex Wilson, shows up dead at his home.

Gathering the remaining jurors at the police station, Holmes favours the injured Jeremy Lopez as the killer, but, to his surprise, Lopez has no problem in supplying a sample of his DNA.

The blood at the Guthrie murder scene is found to belong to army chaplain Audrey Higuerra. But she's been in Kabul for the past three weeks.

Watson cracks the case when she discovers that Audrey was active in assisting leukaemia patients, having donated bone marrow. Jeremy Lopez, a former sufferer, received bone marrow from Audrey and, as a result, the DNA in his blood belongs to her. His saliva, however, contains his own DNA, which is why he had no problem providing a sample.

The best and the wisest man: Holmes is initially confident that he can deduce how the Leviathan was cracked within a matter of hours; after 17 of those hours have elapsed, he attacks the safe with an axe in frustration. He's figured out the lock code on Watson's cellphone. He makes her breakfast but he's also estimated how long it will take her to consume it, shower and get dressed. He's proficient on the piano (just like the Holmes in Josh Friedman's pilot script), playing while chatting to Gregson in Justin Guthrie's apartment. He praises Joan to the skies in front of her family, telling her later, "I meant very little of what I said."

I am lost without my Boswell: Joan dresses very primly to join her mother for brunch. Her brother Oren is involved in a relationship with a woman named Gabrielle. Using Watson's cellphone, Holmes arranges a family get-together and blackmails her into taking him along. He regales the Watson clan with the story of the episode *Power Play*. Joan's mother visits the brownstone at the end of the episode to say that she believes Joan would be happier as a detective than as a sober companion.

The efficiency of our detective police force: Gregson is bemused when Holmes and Watson return Le Chevalier's stolen goods, but knows enough not to ask how they came by these art treasures.

Bell is present, but again has so little to contribute that the producers might just as well have given him the week off.

There is a strong family resemblance about misdeeds: Joan's mother is named Mary (although she's never addressed as such onscreen). In the Canon, the doctor's first wife was, of course, Mary Morstan.

Holmes' famous line makes its first appearance in the series: "When you've eliminated the impossible," he tells

Watson, "whatever remains, however improbable, is the truth."

"I know, Watson, that you share my love of all that is bizarre and outside the humdrum routine of ordinary life," is a quote from *The Red-Headed League*.

The bone marrow clue is very similar to a plot point in an early Patricia Cornwell novel.

I have never loved: Holmes has, apparently been "studying" female twins Gwen and Olivia Lynch in his bedroom. Watson must be a heavy sleeper. When the doorbell rings during the final scene, Joan suggests it might be triplets.

A seven-per-cent solution: Watson accuses Holmes of indulging in the obsessions of addiction without taking drugs.

She threatens him with a drug test when he disturbs her sleep playing *Ode to Joy* at 3AM.

He blackmails her into taking him along on her dinner with her family by saying he is feeling "relapse-y."

Holmes' grateful employers send him several $500 bottles of champagne, which Joan pours down the sink (she never thought to give them to her family?).

Joan's mother mentions Liam, who made an appearance in the previous episode.

A certain unexpected vein of pawky humour: Holmes, as per usual, outrages Watson by smashing the glass covering a lithograph in Peter Kent's home.

Seeing evidence of Audrey Higuerra's entirely blameless life, Holmes remarks: "If I could attribute three miracles to her, I'd nominate her for sainthood."

A running gag about Holmes believing himself to be the smartest man in the world ends with him refuting that assertion. When Watson points out that he is being uncommonly modest, he replies, "There's just no reliable way to test the hypothesis."

Watson: "Someone once said, once you've eliminated the impossible, whatever remains, no matter how improbable, is the truth." Holmes: "Sounds like a windbag."

My head is in a whirl: Why is Holmes allowed to play the piano in Justin Guthrie's apartment? Are Gregson and Bell not even entertaining the notion of fingerprints? Speaking of which, we see a close up of Holmes' bare hands as he plays, but when he rises from the piano he's wearing gloves.

"People find their paths in the strangest of ways." It's no surprise to us that Holmes and Watson will eventually end up working together, but this is the first episode to signpost that outcome. It's surprising, perhaps a little disappointing, that more isn't done with the Le Chevalier angle (which is the primary focus of the episode's promo). As it is, the promising notion of a master thief hiding in plain sight as one of New York's cultural elite is dismissed almost as quickly as it is raised. This episode marks the second time Holmes has visited Sing Sing Prison, the first being in *One Way to Get Off*.

1X11: Dirty Laundry
US Airdate: 3 January 2013

Writers: Liz Friedman & Christopher Silber
Director: John David Coles

Guest Cast: Jake Weber (Geoffrey Silver); Mark Moses (Oliver Purcell); Melissa Farman (Carly Purcell); Leigh Ann Larkin (Harmony); Cynthia Darlow (Mrs Dean); Sam Freed (Oliver's Lawyer); Simon Jutras (French Businessman); Arash Mokhtar (Middle Eastern Diplomat #1); Al Nazemian (Middle Eastern Diplomat #2); Jennifer Regan (Agent Claudia Camden); Shirley Roeca (Estella); Natalie Toro (Marisol); Beau Allen (Businessman); Nicole J Casseri-Healey (High End Escort); Tracey Ruggiero (Terri Purcell)*

*Uncredited

Plot: The body of Terri Purcell, general manager of a swanky New York hotel, is found dumped in a washing machine. A pen is found with the body, but there are no traces of ink.

Holmes deduces that Terri's husband Oliver is sleeping apart from his wife, his joblessness having created a rift between them. He has an alibi for the night of Terri's death. Joan forms a bond with the Purcell's daughter, Carly.

A nosey neighbour informs Holmes and Watson that Terri was often visited by charity worker and family friend Geoffrey Silver. Much to Holmes' annoyance, he too has an alibi.

Informed by Detective Bell that the hotel had a problem with prostitutes, Holmes and Watson are surprised to learn that Terri actively assisted the hookers to ply their trade, introducing them to visiting UN diplomats.

Discovering hidden cameras within the hotel rooms, Holmes suggests to Gregson that Terri may have been blackmailing her guests. He examines many hours of footage, but the most incriminating images are hidden within Terri's family album – recordings made not made for blackmail purposes, but for those of espionage. The Purcells were Russian spies, and Holmes believes that Geoffrey Silver was their handler. Silver won't admit to his part in the conspiracy, but Oliver confesses, and claims he didn't want their daughter to go into the family business.

Meeting privately with Joan, Carly admits to attacking and killing Terri, after learning the life her mother had planned out for her. But the evidence of Terri's autopsy shows that she fought back, something Carly failed to mention. Holmes realises that Terri was not actually dead after Carly attacked her. Silver killed Terri in order to trick the teenager into joining his spy program, by making her believe she'd killed her own mother. The pen found at the scene of the crime was a spy gadget filled with invisible ink – under fluorescent light, Terri's hand-print appears on Silver's shirt, proof that they fought after Carly thought her mother dead.

The best and the wisest man: Holmes offers Watson the position of apprentice and suggests that she begin to take notes. He once spent an afternoon searching a Queen Anne secretary for secret compartments. His multiple TV viewing exercise (as seen in the pilot episode and *The Long Fuse*) comes in handy when reviewing Terri's incriminating tapes. Having run out of plates, he's taken to eating pasta out of mugs. He makes a vague reference to TV spy comedy *Get Smart* (and yet, a few episodes later, he doesn't appear to know who Columbo is – to an

Englishman, the cop in the mac is far better known than Maxwell Smart). This episode marks the first time he addresses his colleague as "My dear Watson."

I am lost without my Boswell: Joan is adamant that she will not be working as Holmes' apprentice. She gives Carly Purcell her number and is happy to talk her through her difficulties (not realising just how difficult those difficulties might be). She blames Silver for ruining Carly's life. Later, she applies Holmes' method by pinning the evidence in the case on her bedroom wall, and requests Terri Purcell's autopsy report. At the end of the episode, she tells Holmes she'll be starting work with a new client in a week.

The efficiency of our detective police force: Gregson doesn't relish the prospect of putting teams of officers to work examining the incriminating videotapes. He displays a particular dislike of Jeffrey Silver.
Once again, Bell is largely overlooked.

There is a strong family resemblance about misdeeds: Foreign spies turn up in *The Second Stain* and *The Bruce-Partington Plans*, but there are no distinct similarities between this episode and anything in the Canon.

I have never loved: Holmes is not subtle in suggesting that Terri and Silver may have been having an affair.
He has no difficulty in spotting a high-end prostitute; Joan thinks this ability misogynistic, not the last time she will accuse him of this trait.

A seven-per-cent solution: Having taken a personal inventory, Holmes has determined that he is "excelling" in his recovery.

Carly confesses to having had a problem with painkillers.

A certain unexpected vein of pawky humour: Holmes is counting down the time until Joan leaves, accurate to the minute. To her bewilderment and embarrassment, he addresses a prostitute with the line, "My friend and I were wondering what you might charge to sleep with us."

He challenges Joan's assertion than his untidiness might be a sign of relapse by emptying out the neighbours' bins in his TV room. "I've been sitting here for hours, but I haven't felt any additional temptation to use drugs."

The promo deliberately alters the sequence in which Holmes examines Terri's encrypted videos and warns Watson that "whatever's on these videos is likely to be the vilest and most startling material that Mrs Purcell gathered." Instead of mundane footage of guests in conversation (as it is in the episode), we see a clip of a cute kitten. Watson responds: "Wow, I don't know how I'm ever going to unsee that."

My head is in a whirl: Once again, an intelligent killer, in this case a professional spy, makes an obvious mistake. Why didn't Geoffrey Silver dispose of the pen, instead of leaving it with Terri's body? He knew full well that the ink had stained his shirt. Come to that, how often does he change his clothes? He's still wearing the same shirt when he's interrogated, several days after the murder.

For some reason, the hotel around which much of the plot revolves doesn't appear to have a name.

"The only promise a puzzle makes is an answer." The first episode after the mid-season hiatus is a rather muted affair, but it would hardly have been fair to uninitiated viewers to begin with the atypical *M*. It's far from clear at this point, but big changes are on the way.

1X12: M
US Airdate: 10 January 2013

Writer: Robert Doherty
Director: John Polson

Guest Cast: Bobb'e J Thompson (Teddy); Marsha Stephanie Blake (Melanie Cullen); Mark Morettini (Uniformed Cop); Gabrielle Senn (Escort); Roman Blat (Orderly)*; Robert Lee Harvey (Ian Vickers)*

*Uncredited

Plot: Gregson summons Holmes and Watson to a crime scene with a lot of blood but no body. Ian Vickers has vanished from his home, and Holmes has no hesitation in identifying the crime as the work of a serial killer known only as M, who has been active in the UK for the last ten years.

Though Holmes claims the murderer has no particular grudge against him, M nevertheless leaves a threatening letter for him in the brownstone. Holmes reluctantly admits to Joan that, a year and a half earlier, M was responsible for killing Irene Adler, and that he intends to exact revenge rather than turn the serial killer over to the NYPD.

Beating the cops to the scene of M's next crime, the home of Melanie Cullen, Holmes subdues the killer and takes him to a secret location, planning to torture and murder him. But M – alias former marine Sebastian Moran – claims to have been in Brixton Prison at the time Irene was murdered in her flat in Camden Lock. He insists that he didn't even know Holmes was living in New York or that the brownstone was his address, He believes he's being framed by his employer. Moran isn't a serial killer, but an assassin, working on the orders of a master criminal called Moriarty, who sends Moran his orders in coded form via cellphone.

Joan realises that Moran is being held prisoner at one of his father's other New York properties, but by the time Gregson arrives there, Holmes has already turned the killer over to the police.

The best and the wisest man: Preparing for Watson's departure, Holmes plans to turn her bedroom into an indoor apiary. He has come to view their relationship as a crutch, and tells her that he's invigorated by the serial killer case only because he failed to capture M in Britain. Without Watson's knowledge, he has installed hidden security cameras within the brownstone (taking a lesson from Terri Purcell?). He doesn't remove them as a result of Joan's outrage, either - he uses them to establish an alibi for himself in the very next episode. His father's first initial is also M – we see his name on the report Joan is struggling to write. It's obviously an attempt to put the viewer on the wrong scent. Holmes' father is unnamed in the Canon, but W S Baring-Gould speculated that his name may have been Siger, given that, according to *The Empty House*, Holmes adopted the identity Sigerson when travelling the world while presumed dead (Siger's son, get it?). That fact that Moran is an Arsenal fan is, for Holmes, yet another reason to despise him. He considers using his bees against Moran, but fears that an allergy might kill him instantly (this angle reappears in the episode *A Landmark Story*, as does Moran himself). Holmes eventually apologises to Joan for lying to her.

I am lost without my Boswell: Watson wants to perform "exit protocols" with her client. She sees her own therapist, who, like Joan's mother, also suggests Joan should consider working as an investigator (though she changes her tune quite dramatically a few episodes down the line). Joan admits to Holmes that she'll miss working with him. "I think what you do is amazing," she tells him, as they examine the corpse of Ian Vickers. He repeats her words after Moran's arrest. She is, though, understandably angry when she discovers his hidden surveillance cameras. She asks Holmes Sr to allow her to stay on for a while, given the traumatic experience his son has just undergone. He refuses, but she lies to Sherlock, stating that she has been given permission to remain.

The efficiency of our detective police force: Gregson places officers outside Holmes' brownstone, and is stunned by the consultant's refusal to go into protective custody after Moran breaks into the building under the noses of the cops. He's mad as hell when Joan tells him about Holmes' plans, admitting that he too has felt the desire for revenge, but has always restrained himself.

Bell is the one who locates the building in which Holmes is keeping Moran prisoner.

There is a strong family resemblance about misdeeds:
This is the first episode of *Elementary* to mention both Holmes' famous arch-enemy, Moriarty and his right-hand man, Sebastian Moran, who appears in the story *The Empty House*, set three years after the Professor's death. In the Canon, he's a crack shot, not a sadistic killer. Holmes describes him as "the second most dangerous man in London."

Holmes deduces that Moran is staying in one of the Betancourt chain of hotels. John Gregory Betancourt is the author responsible for the 1996 pastiche *The Adventure of the Amateur Mendicant Society*.

I have never loved: Like Holmes, Moran also favours the company of prostitutes, but not when he's trying to watch Arsenal.

One of Holmes' informants, Teddy, mistakes Joan for a hooker.

Holmes claims to have been "smitten" with Irene, though the fact that he is intent upon committing murder to avenge her loss indicates somewhat stronger emotions.

A seven-per-cent solution: Holmes tells Watson that his addiction made it impossible for him to capture M in London. What he fails to mention is that he became an addict following Irene's death.

A certain unexpected vein of pawky humour: Holmes: "Reflection is for mirrors, can't you just hand me a report card?" Apart from that, an episode in which a sadistic killers drains his victims of their blood is, unsurprisingly, laugh-free. Why not make up for this deficit by trying to work out which episode title becomes more amusing with the addition of the phrase "in my pants"? My candidate would be *You Do It To Yourself*.

My head is in a whirl: Holmes Sr's text to Joan tells her to expect her "final check", rather than, as an Englishman would write it, "cheque."

We never find out why Moriarty wants Ian Vickers or Melanie Cullen dead.

The cops watching the brownstone do a pretty sloppy job, if they didn't consider that M might enter via the back door.

"He presumed to know me. He needed to be shown that he did not." A game-changing story, and not simply because it's the second episode in two weeks to contain the word "bollocks." That said, it's not as though there aren't a few more lacklustre episodes to come, and the lack of any mystery component in the story is regrettable. Vinnie Jones is suitably menacing as the stone-cold killer, but good luck to anyone who can seriously believe in him as a Sebastian.

1X13: The Red Team
US Airdate: 31 January 2013

Writer: Jeffrey Paul King
Story: Jeffrey Paul King & Craig Sweeny
Director: Christine Moore

Guest Cast: Richard Bekins (Harold Dresden); Michael Laurence (Walter McClenahan); Chris Sullivan (Todd Clarke); Tawny Cypress (Black Suit); Kelly AuCoin (Grey Suit); Clifton Duncan (Uniform #1); Tom Riis Farrell (Gary Sullivan); Philip Hernandez (Carlo Anillo); Robert C Kirk (Detective Harris); Reese Madigan (Sheldon Frost); Kathryn Meisle (Therapist); Nancy Ringham (Sheila Dresden); Ann Sanders (Veena Mehta); Jessica Shea Alverson (Blonde Victim)*

*Uncredited

Plot: Holmes summons Watson to the home of Len Ponticorvo, AKA Zapruder, moderator of Swirltheory.com, a popular website among conspiracy theorists. Len hasn't been heard of in some days, and while his colleagues suspect a sinister motive behind his silence, Holmes thinks he may have suffered a heart attack. He's quite wrong, however – Ponticorvo is found hanged. Examining the terrarium of the victim's pet tortoise, Clyde, Holmes discovers a hidden listening device.

Studying Len's files, he comes across one theory he doesn't consider completely laughable: The Red Team, a group of civilian experts formed to simulate terrorist attacks upon the United States. The findings of the 2009 Red Team are classified. Could they have discovered a flaw in America's national security? At least one member of the team is already dead.

The trail leads to a long-term care facility in Queens – Carlo Anillo was admitted with Alzheimer's; Holmes is convinced he's another member of the team, and that his condition if the result of a poison derived from rotten shellfish.

The murder investigation grinds to a halt when a fellow conspiracy nut Gary Sullivan confesses to killing Ponticorvo following a row over the moon landings.

Gregson gradually accepts Holmes' theory and has all the members of the Red Team rounded up. All refuse to co-operate, but one leaves behind a note instructing them to locate an army captain who went by the code name Yossarian.

Holmes believes Todd Clark, who has been keeping Len Ponticorvo's home under surveillance, to be Yossarian. But Clark is been shot dead, and the detective instructs Bell to put all the surviving members of the Red Team under protective custody in an hotel.

It starts to look as though one member, Walter McClenahan, is attempting to do away with the others. Another expert, Harold Dresden, shares Holmes' suspicions, and intimates that McClenahan is attempting to drive up the price of the information they discovered by killing his colleagues. Bell, however, discovers McClenahan dead, and Holmes realises that Dresden is the real killer, killing or silencing his fellows to prevent the plan from leaking to foreign powers or terrorist organizations. Holmes convinces Dresden that he has deduced the Red Team's plan and that the secret is already spreading. Believing that to be the case, Dresden has no option but to give himself up.

The best and the wisest man: Holmes finds cleanliness disorientating. He's gone without sleep for five nights, amassing information on the shadowy Moriarty, after which he slept for two days. He considers conspiracy theories "pure sophistry," and takes delight in toying with enthusiasts via Swirltheory.com. He quotes Ralph Waldo Emerson: "Consistency is the hobgoblin of little minds." He lies about his NYPD credentials in order to question Carlo Anillo. He enjoys listening to static on the radio, finding it conducive to thought. He has no intention of apologising to Gregson for his actions in the previous episode. He carries a whistle, which he attempts to use to hail a New York cab (in *Snow Angels*, he blows it simply to draw attention). He comes up with the Red Team's secret on the spur of the moment. Luckily, he's right. "A gun to one's head is a very powerful stimulus," he explains.

I am lost without my Boswell: Joan still hasn't told Holmes that she is no longer his official sober companion. She diagnoses Carlo Anillo's seizure, the sign that he does not, in fact, have Alzheimer's. Her car, last seen in the pilot episode, is clearly long gone; she and Holmes conduct a surveillance in a rental vehicle.

The efficiency of our detective police force: Following the events of *M*, Gregson has, understandably, suspended Holmes. He won't listen to Joan's pleas because he doubts his former advisor is even sorry for what happened with Moran (he's quite correct, of course), and is displeased to discover Holmes in an interrogation room with Gary Sullivan. He favours a bar called McNab's. It's there that he reluctantly reinstates Holmes, but not before punching him in the gut.

Bell attempts, without success to persuade Holmes to stay away from the scene of Zapruder's murder. Plainly, he isn't trying all that hard, or he could simply have ordered uniformed officers to escort Holmes and Watson off the property or have them arrested for interfering in a police investigation. (see **My head is in a whirl**). By the latter part of the episode, he isn't even trying, welcoming Holmes to the scene of Walter McClenahan's murder.

There is a strong family resemblance about misdeeds: In the opening shot, we see that Holmes has collected a variety of clippings and pinned them up around the name "Moriarty" (in a fashion not dissimilar to Robert Downey Jr's wall of evidence in *Sherlock Holmes: A Game of Shadows*, in fact). Among them is a drawing of Napoleon Bonaparte. In *The Final Problem*, Holmes memorably described his adversary as "the Napoleon of crime."

Holmes' casual mistreatment of Clyde the tortoise recalls the multiple "deaths" of Watson's dog Gladstone in the Downey Jr/Law movies.

Is the Red Team a vague nod to *The Red-Headed League*? Probably not.

Todd Clark's code name, Yossarian, is, of course, drawn from Joseph Heller's novel *Catch-22*.

I have never loved: The only heartfelt relationship in this episode is between Harold Dresden and his disabled wife, Sheila. He tells Holmes that he would have sold his secrets if he truly believed a foreign power might be able to cure her.

A seven-per-cent solution: Joan's own therapist warns her that she might be the catalyst for a relapse, should Holmes discover that she's been lying to him. Watson has convinced herself that she's only staying on at the brownstone until she can persuade Gregson to take Holmes on as an advisor once more.

Holmes introduces his companion with the words "This

is Joan Watson; she keeps me from doing heroin."

Despite Joan's absence at the climax, he forgoes alcohol from the minibar in Dresden's hotel room. He's uncomfortable visiting Gregson's bar of choice.

A certain unexpected vein of pawky humour: Holmes on conspiracy theorists: "I adore them, as one would a barmy uncle, or a pet that can't stop walking into walls."

He and Joan battle over the fate of Len's tortoise Clyde (surely the breakout TV performance of 2013): Holmes wants to turn the creature into soup stock, and uses him as a paperweight in the meantime. He eventually sits down to a bowl of split pea soup, concluding that Clyde is too magnificent to eat. This third member of the crime-busting team makes a very gradual reappearance in the episode *Snow Angels*.

Gregson and Bell share an amusing scene, with Holmes stage-managing affairs via phone. "It'd probably be easier to fire the guy if we ever actually paid him," Bell concludes.

My head is in a whirl: Bell simply allows Holmes, a man recently suspended from a position with the NYPD for kidnapping and torturing a suspect, to walk away from a crime scene with the victim's files, tortoise, and a recently-discovered bugging device?

Having closed the case on Len Ponticorvo's murder and thrown Holmes out of the station house, why do the cops conduct a tox screen on Carlo Anillo?

"I'm smarter than everyone I meet, Watson. I know it's bad form to say that, but in my case, it's a fact; allowances have to be made." The climax of this episode is bound to disappoint. It's ultimately a big tease – we're never going to find out what the Red Team discovered and what Holmes subsequently deduces. Had the scriptwriter truly come up with an infallible method of outwitting homeland security, he could probably do more with it than use it as a gimmick in an hour-long segment of a CBS crime drama. The issue of Holmes and Watson spending sufficient screen time together has been solved by this point. Oddly, although the show has no narrator, it seems to be Joan's lot in this episode to begin each scene with an explanation of where she and Holmes are, and what has led them there.

1X14: The Deductionist
US Airdate: 3 February 2013

Writer: Craig Sweeny & Robert Doherty
Director: John Polson

Guest Cast: Terry Kinney (Martin Ennis); Kari Matchett (Kathryn Drummond); Jessica Hecht (Patricia Ennis); David Wilson Barnes (Cooper); Roger Robinson (Bruce Kushner); Napiera Groves (Sexy Woman #1); Scott Jaeck (Maxwell Krebs); Che Ayende (Vasquez); Whitney Kimball Long (Sophie); Christopher Burns (Detective); Elizabeth Masucci (Sexy Woman #2); Nikiya Mathis (Nurse); Scott Whitehurst (Doctor); Jesse Hochmuth (Reggie); Elizabeth Ariosto (Cindy); Jason Babinsky (Uniformed Cop #1)*; Nadir Hasan (Orderly)* Jesse Lenat (Homeless Man)*; Kohler McKenzie (Uniformed Cop #2)*; Gil O'Brien (Orderly)*

*Uncredited

Plot: Convicted serial killer Howard Ennis, AKA The Peeler, escapes from hospital as he is preparing for the kidney transplant that will save the life of his sister Patricia.

Kathryn Drummond, the FBI profiler responsible for Ennis' capture is brought in on the case. But Ennis goes out of his way not to kill a young woman in a holdup at a 7/11, determined to show that Kathryn's theories about him are incorrect. In her book on Ennis, she alleged that his father abused him, a charge that led to the suicides of both parents.

Watson realises that Patricia deliberately destroyed her kidneys, necessitating her brother's temporary release from prison. Patricia is visited in hospital by Kathryn, who confesses that she falsified the claims of sexual abuse in her book. Holmes' warning to Detective Bell comes too late to prevent Patricia stabbing Kathryn.

When her brother telephones Gregson, Holmes is able to pinpoint his location by tracing the source of the radio stations to which he is listening. He confronts Ennis alone, overpowers him, and hands him over to the police.

The best and the wisest man: Holmes claims – probably in jest – that he was once robbed by a man in his underwear. As in *Rat Race*, he again escapes from handcuffs. He considers serial killers duller than the Queen's jubilee (a topical reference at the time of broadcast). He says "bollocks" once again – you can get a lot of mileage out of a swear when no-one in the country knows what it means, so listen out for it again in the episodes *A Landmark Story* and *Heroine*. Just as he took offence to Moran presuming to know him, he bears a particular resentment for Kathryn Drummond after she published a thinly-veiled depiction of him in an article entitled *The Deductionist*. He stabbed Moran for his presumption, but here it's Ennis' ailing sister who attacks Kathryn. Holmes' language growing more archaic still, he refers to prostitutes as "dollymops."

I am lost without my Boswell: To Holmes' bemusement, Joan still maintains her apartment, returning to it whenever she's not working as a sober companion. She discovers that her sublessor has filmed a pornographic film in her apartment, rendering her couch no longer fit for purpose. Faced with eviction, she spots evidence in the video that proves it was made with the knowledge and approval of Bruce the landlord. She leaves the despoiled apartment anyway.

The efficiency of our detective police force: Gregson is exasperated by the fact that Ennis refuses to act in the way predicted by both Holmes and Kathryn, the attack on whose life occurs right under Bell's nose.

There is a strong family resemblance about misdeeds: This is the first time Holmes is seen practising his singlestick technique. In Chapter Two of *A Study in Scarlet*, Watson notes that Holmes is "an expert singlestick player," causing many to believe that it might be some sort of musical instrument. It is, in fact, a form of fencing in which a length of wood, rather than a blade, is the weapon. Holmes is never seen to wield a singlestick anywhere in the Canon, making this a particularly obscure reference.

I have never loved: The episode begins with two scantily-clad prostitutes performing a dance routine for a seated Holmes before handcuffing him and proceeding to steal his valuables. It's all a trap, of course, and the cops are waiting to arrest them.

He watches the porno filmed in Joan's apartment and finds it mundane and riddled with continuity errors. He notes that her spatula has been desecrated and intimates that something similar may have been done to her toothbrush at the brownstone (by the dollymops?).

A seven-per-cent solution: In her article, *The Deductionist*, Kathryn correctly anticipates Holmes' problems with addiction.

A certain unexpected vein of pawky humour: "This place still smells like stripper," Joan complains, the night after his spectacular bust (fner fner).

Most of the humour in the episode is derived from Holmes' past relationship with Kathryn. Joan: "I know why you don't like her." Holmes: "You recall my aversion to bile-spewing pig-women?" When Joan concludes that she was an ex, Holmes replies: "More of a C+ at best." And then there's the porn movie...

My head is in a whirl: The credits list Ennis' first name as Martin, but he is referred to as Howard throughout the episode.

Ennis is captured by the hoariest of cop show clichés, tuning in his radio while telephoning the cops. And why does he call Gregson, anyway? In fact, the whole plan doesn't really make sense, given that the perfectly healthy brother, an experienced killer, is required only to publicly avoid killing in order to show Kathryn up, while Patricia's part of the plan necessitates her ruining her own kidneys. What was stopping her from killing Kathryn while Howard was behind bars?

Kathryn's article predicts Holmes' descent into drug addiction, but this occurred only because of the murder of his one true love. Did she also foresee the existence and subsequent death of someone like Irene?

"I want to see if either of us can be more than our profile." It's odd that this distinctly humdrum episode was selected to follow the Superbowl, a prestigious slot on US television (the promo features Holmes and Watson watching the game). Miller and Liu are on good form, but Kathryn's character becomes irrelevant the moment she's stabbed by Patricia. The fact that Joan is given her own distinct subplot again, a standby of the early episodes, suggests there's really not enough going on this week.

1X15: A Giant Gun, Filled With Drugs
US Airdate: 7 February 2013

Writers: Corinne Brinkerhoff & Liz Friedman
Story: Christopher Silber
Director: Guy Ferland

Guest Cast: John Hannah (Rhys Kinlan); Michael Irby (Xande Diaz); Armand Schultz (Derrick Hughes); Allie Gallerani (Emily Grant); Joey Auzenne (Delivery Guy); Herman Chavez (Dominican Painter #1); Chris Nuñez (DJ)*; Mauricio Ovalle (Reynaldo)*

*Uncredited

Plot: Emily Grant, the daughter of Holmes' former drug dealer Rhys Kinlan, is abducted from her New York home. The kidnappers are demanding the $2.2m Rhys stole from his Dominican suppliers. But most of the money is gone, and Rhys has no-one else to turn to but his old friend and most valued customer.

A smudge left on the wall of Emily's home leads to a Dominican-themed nightclub, Hurrikane, where Rhys recognises Renaldo, an old enemy. Holmes identifies one of Renaldo's men, Xande Diaz, as an undercover DEA agent. Diaz insists that the cartel has nothing to do with Emily's abduction.

Emily's Tweets suggest that her father-in-law Derrick Hughes recently asked her for money, and Holmes discovers that she's been writing cheques to Derrick, a former real estate ace turned hard-up car park attendant. Tracking him from his place of work, Holmes thinks he's discovered the home where he's been keeping his stepdaughter captive, but Hughes has nothing to do with the kidnapping – he's simply squatting in one of his old properties.

Angered that Rhys has involved Holmes, the kidnapper reduces the time he has to deliver the ransom money, and sends a box containing Emily's severed finger to the brownstone. The clues Holmes discovers on it are not enough in themselves to indicate her whereabouts. In desperation, he requests a loan from his father in order to pay the ransom.

When making the money drop, Holmes realises he has walked into an ambush. DEA agent Diaz arrives at the brownstone, and holds Joan and Rhys hostage – he's the real kidnapper, and speaking to Holmes over the phone, he demands that the detective transfer the money into his account. Rhys breaks free of his bonds, and is shot. Joan knocks Diaz out with Holmes' phrenology bust.

Under interrogation, Diaz at first denies all knowledge of Emily's kidnapping, but later capitulates when Gregson and Bell make it clear that Holmes has sufficient evidence to locate his hiding place, an empty pre-war building near his apartment.

The best and the wisest man: Holmes doesn't deny that Rhys is a trigger "on a giant gun, filled with drugs" (hence the rather unwieldy episode title) but is satisfied – at first – that he can assist his old friend without succumbing. He considers Emily's Twitter feed "suffocatingly inane" and "soul-crushing in its utter banality." He has only one camera outside the house, and apparently still hasn't removed the ones indoors. He knows how to hot-wire a vehicle. His father remains unseen and, even though they communicate telephonically in this episode, unheard. He insists that he could eventually locate Emily, but doesn't want to spend any more time than is necessary in Rhys' company. He informs his ex-dealer that their friendship is at an end. He returns his father's money, but pays Rhys from his own funds to get out of his life.

I am lost without my Boswell: Joan again accuses Holmes of misogyny when he tells her that he has worked out her menstrual cycle. She's in full sober companion mode here, insisting that they attend daily AA meetings while Rhys is staying in the brownstone. She's entirely prepared to turn Rhys over to the cops if she feels her partner's sobriety has been compromised. She remembers that Holmes calls his phrenology bust Angus (a fact revealed in *Child Predator*).

The efficiency of our detective police force: This is a largely cop-free episode, given that communicating with the official forces will result in Emily's death. Acting unofficially, Bell supplies Holmes with information of Emily's stepfather. If this episode were set after *Details*, it would seem that he's returning a favour. But it's not, so that's that. He and Gregson interrogate Diaz at the episode's climax, the first time that neither Holmes or Watson have sat in on the questioning of the guilty party.

There is a strong family resemblance about misdeeds: Holmes' first appearance in the episode has him relating the events of *The Crooked Man* to a gathering of fellow addicts. He plans to tell them the story of *The Blue Carbuncle* at the next meeting.
  "I can identify 140 cigarette and cigar brands by their ash alone," He boasts, referencing a similar claim in *The Boscombe Valley Mystery*. "If you'd bother to read my monograph, you'd know that." The ash distinction discussion also shows up in the *Sherlock* episode *A Scandal in Belgravia*.
  The severed finger in the box discovered at the back door of the brownstone is perhaps a nod to *The Cardboard*

Box (in which the body parts are ears).

In a rare acknowledgement of the BBC's *Sherlock*, both Rhys and Joan say "I believe in Sherlock Holmes," a reference to the tiresome internet meme that resulted from the final episode of Season Two.

I have never loved: Rhys makes the assumption that Joan is Holmes' "bird." Big mistake.

A seven-per-cent solution: Joan notes that his *Crooked Man* recollection is the first time he's contributed at a meeting.

Rhys once delivered drugs to Holmes at Scotland Yard. He also provided him with cocaine during a locked room mystery known as the Tinsdale case. Rhys again tempts Holmes with coke, but instead of accepting, he attacks the dealer.

He's surprisingly eager to attend another meeting at the case's conclusion: "Others may find inspiration in my abstinence... apparently"

A certain unexpected vein of pawky humour: Joan is to say the least unsettled at discovering a naked Rhys on the landing of the brownstone.

Holmes knows that asking his father for the ransom money will cost him something in return: "stealing candy from infants, or clubbing young seals."

The CBS promo is, as usual, heavy on humour, but actually contains very little material from this episode.

My head is in a whirl: Hurrikane is one of those nightclubs only seen on TV, where the music isn't so loud you can't hear yourself talk, and filled with only as many revellers as the budget will run to.

Holmes says that Emily's stepfather is named Derrick

Hughes, but one scene later, Bell refers to him as Derrick *Hume*.

Having made it plain that Joan mistrusts Rhys, it's odd that she should leave him alone with Holmes at a café table while she orders some food. In fact, given her mistrust of the man, why doesn't she subject him to the same drug tests she gave Holmes in early episodes?

"We have just under 44 hours until the ransom is due – luxury. That's twice what I'll need." The episode is less interesting for its plot or for its depiction of Holmes' temptation than it is for the character of Rhys Kinlan, a scumbag through and through. He doesn't know what illness killed Emily's mother, and even though he's concerned about his daughter's fate, he just can't stop himself from trying to ply Holmes with drugs – it's simply in his nature to act in this fashion, and well-drawn though he is, we can only hope that, for Holmes' sake, we'll never see him again in *Elementary*.

1X16: Details
US Airdate: 14 February 2013

Writers: Jeffrey Paul King & Jason Tracey
Story: Robert Doherty
Director: Sanaa Hamri

Guest Cast: Malcolm Goodwin (Andre Bell); Paula Graces (Officer Paula Reyes); Anwan Glover (Curtis Bradshaw); Lynda Gravatt (Lenore); Michael Bakkensen (Reporter #1); Matt McGorry (Officer Sam Klecko); Kelvin McGrue (Cronie #1); Shawn McLean (Cronie #2)

Plot: Driving home at the end of his shift, Bell is shot at by another motorist in a 1968 Chevy Biscayne, wielding an automatic weapon. Escaping relatively unscathed, he has a good idea who wanted to take his life – Curtis Bradshaw, who served a spell in prison thanks to Bell, despite a fellow officer almost jeopardizing the case by attempting to frame the racketeer. Bell recognised the Chevy as the one belonging to Bradshaw, who insists that his vehicle was stolen some days earlier.

After being questioned by Holmes, Bradshaw shows up dead. Holmes identifies prints at the scene of the crime as having been made by Bugatti boots - and Bell happens to own a pair.

Searching Bells' apartment, Holmes discovers a 9mm hidden in the bathroom, and, conducting tests of his own, confirms that it is the gun used to kill Bradshaw. Holmes doesn't tell Gregson about his discovery because he believes someone is attempting to frame Bell.

The incriminating boots were given by the detective to his brother Andre, a former gang member. Andre denies planting the gun, and is later shot in his apartment, writing "was not Marcus" in his own blood.

Another set of incriminating boot-prints is found nearby. Watson realises that it was Bell who blew the whistle on the officer who framed Bradshaw, his former lover Officer Paula Reyes. Holmes identifies her as the killer, and evidence discovered at her home proves her guilt.

The best and the wisest man: Holmes gets to use his American accent for the third time this season, posing as an intruder in the brownstone. Following the climax of the previous episode (which, according to the dialogue, occurred just a week earlier), he's taken to staging surprise "attacks" on Joan in the hope of improving her reactions. He encourages her to take martial arts classes. He also discovered during that last adventure that Joan had chosen to stay with him. That knowledge genuinely affects him, and he virtually pleads with her to join him as his assistant. "I am better with you, Watson," he tells her. "Difficult to say why, exactly. Perhaps in time, I'll solve that as well." His Victorian-era lingo resurfaces, causing him to call a toilet a water closet. He tells Watson that he's assisting Bell because he doesn't want to have to break in another co-operative police officer. He displays his collection of locks by date of manufacture.

I am lost without my Boswell: Visiting her therapist again, Joan describes the events of *A Giant Gun, Filled With Drugs*. Dr Reed is concerned that Joan's life is now potentially at risk – she certainly seems to be letting a lot of his usual social infractions pass without comment these days. Despite the recommendation that she should move on and seek another client, Joan is sufficiently moved by Holmes' speech to agree to live at the brownstone for the foreseeable future, acting as Holmes' partner/apprentice. She likes to be paid on Thursdays.

The efficiency of our detective police force: After too many episodes with too little to do, Bell finally gets a story to himself, and a first name. There's no shortage of people who want him dead, a cause for pride, in Holmes' opinion. After Bradshaw's murder, he's placed on administrative duty.

Gregson never doubts his underling's innocence, though he's anxious that he might be suspected by others.

There is a strong family resemblance about misdeeds: Just as the donation of old clothes to the needy causes problems in *The Hound of the Baskervilles*, so Bell's gift of a pair of Bugatti boots to his needy brother gives the impression that Andre might have killed Bradshaw. In fact, the prints were made by an entirely different pair, purchased by Paula Reyes.

I have never loved: Holmes thinks that Reyes and Bell had sex at least ten times – they were certainly in a close enough relationship for him to give her a key to his home.

Holmes suggests that Reyes teaches Watson to fight. Joan suggests he simply wants to see two women engage in foxy boxing.

A seven-per-cent solution: Holmes suggests that his new working relationship with Watson will relieve her of all confidentiality burdens. She, in turn, insists that he continue to accompany her to AA meetings.

A certain unexpected vein of pawky humour: "Can you think of any reason that Bell would have a lingerie catalogue in which your head has been superimposed on almost all of the models?" Holmes asks Watson after searching the policeman's home. He adds, "He hasn't, but can you think of any reason he would?"

The episode's promo is built around Holmes' mock attempts on Joan's life.

When she sees him conducting ballistics tests in the brownstone, she asks, "Is this another test of my reflexes, because you're about to see how quickly I can call the police."

Holmes' pride is hurt by the fact that he failed to deduce the existence of Bell's brother. When Joan points out that no-one knew, he protests: "Still – I'm me!"

My head is in a whirl: It's fortunate that Holmes volunteers his services in this episode, since it seems unlikely he'd be requested to assist in the case of a drive-by shooting where the identity of the attacker is in little doubt.

Andre wouldn't have been shot if Holmes hadn't shown that someone was attempting to frame his brother. But he doesn't seem to feel any guilt over that, and neither of the Bell brothers holds it against him.

"Nothing makes a smart man stupid like a thirst for vengeance." The turning point in the relationship between Holmes and Watson has finally been reached. Miller's big speech in this episode is brilliantly delivered and genuinely affecting. Their relationship will always be combative, but Holmes has gone from insisting that he doesn't need Watson to acknowledging that he actually does. Dr Candace Reed is starting to look like a possible candidate for Moriarty, but since this episode marks her final appearance in the series, that clearly isn't going to be the case. The mystery itself feels like offcuts from *One Way to Get Off*, since both Gregson and Bell had female colleagues who attempted to frame a criminal when an investigation stalled.

1X17: Possibility Two
US Airdate: 21 February 2013

Writer: Mark Goffman
Director: Seith Mann

Guest Cast: David Furr (Paul Reeves); Christopher Sieber (Carter Lyndon); Albert Jones (Benny Cordero); Jennifer Lim (Natasha Kademan); Gibson Frazier (Raph Keating); Dennis Boutsikaris (Gerald Lydon); Steven Hauck (Crabtree); Michael Izquierdo (Josh Lydon); Caroline Strong (Ashley Mitchell); Tom Galantich (Brian Watt); Barbara Miluski (Agnieszka); Aleksander Mici (Ludoslaw); Patricia Connolly (Greta Dunwoody); Bennett Bradley (Ms Tompkins); George Bartenieff (Jurgi)

Plot: Returning from an easily-resolved shooting case, Holmes and Watson are approached by industrialist Gerald Lydon. He tells them he is suffering from Hereditary CAA, a rare illness of which the first symptom is dementia and the final one is death. But no member of Lydon's family has ever had this condition; he is convinced that he has somehow been given the disorder. Holmes refuses to take the case, believing the most obvious solution – a natural illness – to be the likeliest.

Lydon attempts to bribe the detective with a valuable species of bee. Once again, Holmes declines, but later he receives a call from Captain Gregson – having temporarily lost control of his faculties, Lydon has shot and killed his driver, Crabtree.

Holmes and Watson visit Watt Helix, the genetics company responsible for diagnosing Lydon's CAA. They speak to Raph Keating and his fiancée, Natasha Kademan. Kademan suggests that seven geneticists in the world might be capable of artificially giving someone the condition.

The clues point to a lab in Oslo, where a scientist appears to have been paid off by Gerald Lydon's son Carter. Before Holmes and Watson can pack, they are contacted by Natasha Kademan, who sends them an unlabelled diagram of a molecule. Returning to the Watt Helix lab, they find her murdered.

Keating insists that his fiancée was most likely killed by an ex-con, Benny Cordera, who objected to the tests she conducted upon him. Joan proves that someone may indeed have tampered with Lydon's DNA. But the case falls apart when the blood at the scene of Natasha's murder proves to be a match for Benny Cordera, who insists that on the night she died, he was – for the purposes of blackmail - filming a neighbour engaged in an affair with the nanny.

Holmes finds that Cordera's sample was manufactured by Raph Keating. He believed Natasha was conducting an affair with a Lincoln Dunwoody and confesses to killing her and framing Cordera, but insists he knows nothing of the Gerald Lydon matter.

Holmes discovers that the name of Natasha's supposed lover is in fact the surnames of two wealthy philanthropic families. Unexplained cases of CAA have occurred to members of both the Lincolns and the Dunwoodys. He proves that Brian Watt, semi-retired head of Watt Helix has the same disease, and in order to attract funding for a cure, has induced the condition in some of New York's wealthiest individuals.

The best and the wisest man: At the shooting of two guards employed by ZBZ Security, he pronounces the name "Zed Bee Zed" rather than the American "Zee Bee Zee." He has taken to leaving piles of books outside

Watson's room to assist her in her retraining as a detective. As part of their new arrangement, he tells Watson he will clean out the fridge every month. At one point, he is seen pouring acid onto a child's doll, no doubt in connection with some unrecorded case. He considers utilitarian philosopher Jeremy Bentham the father of modern criminology. Holmes insists that, having first refused it, he has taken Lydon's bee back to the brownstone because he can't refuse a dying man's last wish, but it's hard not to suspect that he just really, really wants the bee. He speaks Norwegian, can pick pockets and has read Natasha Kademan's dissertation, *The Warrior Gene*.

I am lost without my Boswell: In the opening scene, Holmes has a nervous Watson analyse the shooting of the two security guards in Bell's presence. She doesn't consider her first outing as a detective to be a failure (although Holmes ultimately solves the crime), and she does somewhat better in her analysis of the blood spatter at the scene of Natasha Kademan's killing. She later cracks the code of the molecule image Natasha sent them before her murder, and skilfully acquires a sample of Carter Lydon's DNA from a chewed pen. She knows about Hereditary CAA. Her trips to the dry-cleaners to pick up Holmes' sweaters suggest to her that something strange is going on there – little actual cleaning goes on there, and the store boasts an over-abundance of security cameras. He sends her back there when the same sweaters "accidentally" become stained with ink. She eventually realises what Holmes has already deduced: that the dry-cleaners is a front for a money laundering organisation. She informs Bell, who conducts a raid on the premises.

The efficiency of our detective police force: Gregson considers the Lydon case closed, and doubts any connection between the deaths of Crabtree and Kademan. He and Bell interrogate Benny Cordera, but they are constantly interrupted by Holmes texting and hammering on the window.

There is a strong family resemblance about misdeeds: Holmes' name is given to Gerald Lydon by a Mr Musgrave in London. The name is taken from Holmes' university chum and one of his earliest paying clients, seen in *The Musgrave Ritual*.

In *A Study in Scarlet*, Watson considers that Holmes has no knowledge of philosophy, but in the preface to *His Last Bow*, Watson says that Holmes divides his time during his retirement between philosophy and agriculture. Somewhere in between the two lies the truth about his opinion of Jeremy Bentham.

Holmes has a gramophone player, as did his Canonical counterpart in *The Mazarin Stone*.

He encourages Watson to practice with his singlestick.

I have never loved: Holmes prefers to travel to Oslo rather than question Carter Lydon because of his previously undisclosed weakness for Norwegian women.

He suspects that Watson was romantically involved with her insomniac genetics professor, Jerry.

A certain unexpected vein of pawky humour: Holmes tells the cops it's not his place to tell them how to do their job, then – surprise, surprise - proceeds to do just that.

Having ignored Joan's suggestion that he contact the world's top geneticists, he later arranges a video conference with them all, cutting them off before they can reach a conclusion.

Lydon: "I hold 18 patents and I can do 11 pull-ups at age 58." Holmes: "And I own exactly 16 forks. I'm not entirely sure what we're supposed to be comparing."

The promo gives the impression that Holmes accidentally squashes the rare bee, when nothing of the kind happens.

My head is in a whirl: As in *The Red Team*, Holmes is permitted to remove an item from an active crime scene, in this case a box containing a rare species of bee.

Brian Watt has the ability and the resources to create an artificial version of CAA, but not to cure it?

"A good detective knows that every task, every interaction, no matter how seemingly banal, has the potential to contain multitudes. I live my life alert to this possibility. I expect my colleagues to do the same." It's natural to assume that Lydon's shooting of Crabtree will turn out to be a frame-up, and that the testimony of the only witness, a nurse, is a lie. But it's not, and Lydon vanishes from the story after this incident. *Possibility Two* features many of the plot elements familiar from previous episodes, but somehow it fails to gel. Perhaps because the characters are mere pawns at the mercy of the plot, it's hard to really care about anyone, and the one sympathetic character, Gerald Lydon, disappears without trace, his fate uncertain.

1X18: Déjà Vu All Over Again
US Airdate: 14 March 2013

Writer: Brian Rodenbeck
Director: Jerry Levine

Guest Cast: Josh Hamilton (Drew Gardner); Jim True-Frost (Anson Samuels); Geneva Carr (Rebecca Burrell); Andre Royo (Thaddeus); Susan Pourfar (Emily Hankins); Roxanna Hope (Callie Burrell); Timothy Sekk (Ken); Victoria Cartagena (Hope); Kenneth Tigar (Philip Armistead); Penny McNamee (Vivian Tully); Jimmy Palumbo (Security Guard); Stephen Niese (Anchor); David Gibson (Attorney)*

*****Uncredited**

Plot: Holmes' father holds him to the bargain they struck in *A Giant Gun, Filled With Drugs*, and insists that Sherlock assist his colleagues in New York. Attorney Philip Armistead is concerned on behalf of his assistant Rebecca Burrell, whose sister Callie may have been murdered by her husband Drew Gardner six months earlier.

Holmes and Watson view a video in which Callie tells her husband she's leaving him, having been upset by the story of a woman with a bunch of flowers being pushed in front of a subway train. Rebecca is convinced that Drew somehow faked the video and killed his wife.

Watson investigates Callie's disappearance, while Holmes looks into the death of Vivien Tully, the young woman pushed in front of an oncoming subway train. Joan questions Callie's husband, who mentions that the couple split up for a brief period once before. She becomes convinced that Gardner killed Callie. Holmes sends Gardner an anonymous message accusing him of murder, in order to frighten him into action.

Conducting surveillance with Alfredo's assistance, Joan sees Gardner move a large trunk out of a storage locker and believes Callie's body may be inside. She is caught in the act of attempting to break into the trunk, and to make matters worse, she is arrested.

Pursuing the subway murder, Holmes finds that Vivien Tully had a stalker, Anson Samuels, who proves that though he was indeed following her, he didn't push her under a train. But Samuel's video footage shows that a busking musician seems to have followed the pusher after Vivien's death. The performer admits to recognizing the killer as someone whose pocket he had attempted to pick once before.

Disheartened with her failure, Joan plans to tell Rebecca that she cannot continue with the case, when she sees a photograph of Callie wearing her husband's jacket, a jacket that matches the description of the one worn by the man who pushed Vivien Tully under a subway train. But why should Callie be inspired to leave Drew because of her death, and what reason would he have for killing Vivien?

Joan remembers that Drew and Callie were briefly separated eighteen months earlier, which was when she recorded the video in which she mentions the death of the woman with the flowers. At that time, Anna Peters was pushed in front of a train by two brawling students while carrying a bunch of flowers for a sick friend. In order to make it appear that Callie vanished of her own free will, Gardner staged a second murder, matching the accident she described in the video by killing Vivien, thus giving the impression that the video was recorded only six months ago.

The best and the wisest man: Six months have passed

since Holmes and Watson first met. He selected Joan to act as his sober companion, having studied the CVs of several candidates, for reasons that have not yet been determined. He takes an interest in Vivien's death, having lost a valuable informant under similar circumstances in London – he eventually found the killer then, as now. He still refers to the subway as "the tube" (see the pilot episode). He seems not to know who Columbo is. He has many discardable cell phones. "I have the very strongest sensation of déjà vu," he tells Joan when he visits her after her arrest, a callback to the very first episode, in which Holmes found himself incarcerated after wrecking her car. It's heartening that he doesn't mock her, but instead encourages Joan for her boldness.

I am lost without my Boswell: The episode begins with a flashback set just before Watson begins work as Holmes' sober companion. She receives a call from a doctor at Hemdale, who has just sent her Sherlock's case file. Holmes' sponsor Alfredo is teaching her to break into and hot-wire cars. She has yet to identify herself to anyone as a consulting detective. Watson twice forgets her dinner date with an old acquaintance, journalist Emily Hankins. When she finally makes the appointment, she finds a gathering of friends staging an intervention, of which she's organized many in the past. Insulted, she walks out on them. Joan finally cracks the case, and makes her peace with Emily. She alters her professional status on a social networking site from "Sobriety Counselor" to "Consulting Detective."

The efficiency of our detective police force: Gregson doesn't know that Holmes plays the violin, nor has he ever seen him eat.
  Bell accompanies Holmes when he questions the musician. Just like old times.

There is a strong family resemblance about misdeeds: A paraphrased line from *A Study in Scarlet*: "There is no branch of detective work which is as important or as neglected as the art of tracing footsteps." It's a rare thing for the show to quote any story other than the first novel. There are sixty tales to choose from, guys - fill your boots.

A seven-per-cent solution: Holmes knows nothing of the murder of Vivien Tully - he was in Hemdale at the time, without access to newspapers. The crime news overexcited him.

A certain unexpected vein of pawky humour: The CBS promo gives the impression that Watson's attempts at carjacking are comedic, when they're really not.

Holmes gets all the best lines this week: "Opinions are like ani, Watson, everyone has one" and "Have I told you how distracting I find self-doubt? If you must wallow, I ask that you do it in the privacy of your room."

My head is in a whirl: Holmes' phone no longer plays the *Psycho* music when Joan calls, as it did in *One Way to Get Off*, suggesting that it was indeed a cheap gag after all.

And while the ani line is funny, the correct plural is actually "anuses."

We never actually find out what Gardner did with his wife's body.

"It's a case with training wheels." The episode is derived from a line in the movie *Scream*, but the similarity ends there. This is a tightly-constructed mystery with plenty for Watson to do and a thoroughly satisfying solution. It's almost a shame that she and Holmes end up working together in the story quite as soon as they do, since it'd be nice to see her find her way as a detective without any assistance, but it's all part of an arc that works for her character, with her friends questioning her choices and causing her to doubt herself until she cracks the case and gets her name in the papers, which is always nice, unless it relates to public nudity – sorry, Mum.

1X19: Snow Angels
US Airdate: 4 April 2013

Writer: Jason Tracey
Director: Andrew Bernstein

Guest Cast: Jill Flint (Alysa Darwin); Becky Ann Baker (Pam); Frank Wood (EROC Supervisor); Candis Cayne (Ms Hudson); Karl Miller (Squatter); Bill Buell (Private Maggio); Howard McGillin (Davis Renkin); Andy Grotelueschen (Nurse Vince); Christine Rounder (Denise Castor); Curt Bouril (FRP #1); Scott Aiello (Uniform #1); Daniel Loeser (Uniform #2); Slate Holmgren (Uniform #3); Samuel Smith (EMT #1); Nick Sullivan (Frank Dempster); Lonnie Quinn (TV Reporter); Mark Elliot Wilson (Joseph Leseur)

Plot: A blizzard is approaching New York as Holmes and Watson are called to the shooting of a security guard by a group of thieves who were apparently after the latest model of Verzia cellphones. Joan deduces that one of the thieves was also shot in the altercation.

As the power goes out across the city, Denise Castor of FEMA arrives to work alongside the police department. Holmes locates the stolen phones without any difficulty – the thieves dropped them in a dumpster. The phone theft was a ruse – the actual target was a architectural firm in the same building. Blueprints have been stolen.

After a night studying documents, Holmes determines that the criminals are interested in EROC – East Rutherford Operations Centre, a cash depository and processing centre for the Federal Reserve. With no way to contact Gregson, Holmes and Watson hitch a ride to EROC with snow plough driver Pam.

At the facility, they finds that they've arrived too late -

$33m has already been stolen, and the criminals have fled in an ambulance.

Searching for the wounded thief, Bell meets Alysa Darvin as she is about to be released from hospital. She claims she was stabbed by a mugger, but Bell believes her knife injury is actually an attempt to disguise a bullet wound.

The ambulance containing Alysa's fellow thieves and the stolen bills cannot be located, and Holmes suspects that Denise Castor has arranged for it to pass through barriers unobstructed. Gregson fakes a powercut and a riot at the police station, which prompts Denise to attempt to release her co-conspirator. Bell stops them before they even get out of the building.

The best and the wisest man: In a rare show of interest in his own health, Holmes is seen taking cod liver oil. Attempting to save battery power on his cellphone, he uses a magnifying lens during the blackout. "Don't you have an app for that?" Joan asks. She's quite right; we saw it in *Flight Risk*. Holmes neglected to pay the phone bill, and as a result, the service has been disconnected. "In this day and age, a landline is an appendix or a vestigial tail," he insists. He says that the idea behind the heist is so ingenious he'd let the criminals get away with it if they hadn't killed someone. He wonders why Gregson called him in on what appears to be a pretty simple matter.

I am lost without my Boswell: Joan is aggrieved that Holmes is sticking to the letter of their domestic agreement – he cleans the fridge once a month, but does nothing else (clearly, then, *Snow Angels* takes place at least a little over a month after the previous episode). Her detective skills are improving – she realises that the security guard didn't die straight away before even Holmes spots it. From the startled expression on her face, it's plain that Sherlock is lying when he tells an armed man that Joan holds several black belts – his attempts to get her trained in at least one of the martial arts failed, then (file this under **A certain unexpected vein of pawky humour**, too). She initially objects to the presence of Ms Hudson, but later grows to like her.

The efficiency of our detective police force: Bell is seen acting on his own, visiting hospitals in search of the wounded thief. He and Gregson get a few nice scenes working without Holmes and Watson. Bell played Sky Masterson in his high school's production of *Guys and Dolls*. "The stage's loss in New York City's gain," Holmes observes. It's hard to imagine a scenario during which Bell would admit such a thing to Holmes.

There is a strong family resemblance about misdeeds: "Life is infinitely stranger than anything the mind of man could invent," Holmes says, quoting the opening of *A Case of Identity*.

This episode marks the first and only appearance this season of Ms Hudson, this show's equivalent of Baker Street's trusty housekeeper. She's an autodidact and expert in ancient Greek whom Holmes consulted on several cases in London. She's also a pre- or post-op transsexual and an emotional mess. The brownstone looks downright homely once she's had a chance to clean it. Despite the promise that she'll be a semi-regular fixture in the series from now on, she isn't seen for the remainder of the season. Candis Cayne is earnest in the role, though Kristen Johnston of *Third Rock from the Sun* fame might have been more fun in the role. But hey, what do I know?

I have never loved: Holmes has taken Ms Hudson in

following the disintegration of her relationship with Davis Renkin of 3T Enterprises. There's a reconciliation followed by another breakup. Holmes seems oddly edgy when Ms Hudson says she'll see him on Tuesday. What's going on there?

A seven-per-cent solution: Mentions of Holmes' addiction are few and far between now that Watson has taken a new role in his life. Cod liver oil all round, then.

A certain unexpected vein of pawky humour: "Unless the thieves are angling to steal onesies from a Baby Gap, it's very difficult to see what they're after," Holmes complains as he studies duplicates of the stolen blueprints.
When Pam attempts to draw Holmes and Watson into conversation during the long drive to New Jersey, he responds: "We met your price, Pam, I assume it included freedom from small talk." "He gets carsick... like a six year-old," Joan explains.
Clyde the tortoise reappears, a red cross on his back to represent the stolen ambulance in Holmes' reconstruction of the thieves' escape.
Watson: "What if there are 50 commandos shooting up the place?" Holmes: "Well, I have my whistle..."

My head is in a whirl: Joan may wear it well, but is a miniskirt really appropriate clothing for a blizzard?
And while it's one thing for Alysa, locked in an interrogation room, to imagine that there's a riot going on in the police station, how is Denise Castor taken in so thoroughly?

"Well, if I have to solve this in the stone age, I suppose it might be interesting after all." The weather effects, both CGI and practical, are excellent in this episode, convincingly conveying the impression of a blizzard powerful enough to bring the city to a halt. But because we never see the thieves after the pre-credits sequence, or know how close Holmes and Watson are to catching up with them, it's difficult to invest any interest in their crime. Their arrest and the recovery of the money all takes place offscreen, too. Despite the presence of Ms Hudson, snow plough driver Pam interacts with Holmes and Watson far more amusingly. It would be nice to think that we might see her again, as one of Sherlock's NY Irregulars.

1X20: Dead Man's Switch
US Airdate: 25 April 2013

Writers: Liz Friedman & Christopher Silber
Story: Christopher Silber
Director: Larry Teng

Guest Cast: Thomas Jay Ryan (Ken Whitman); Wayne Duvall (Duke Landers); Jospeh Siravo (Anthony Pistone); Thomas Guiry (Brent Garvey); Russell G Jones (Attorney); David Mogentale (Charles Augustus Milverton); Randy Louis Swiren (Stuart Bloom); Portia Reiners (Eva Whitman); Greg Nutcher (Crime Scene Detective)

Plot: Holmes' latest case comes not from Gregson or Bell, but from his sponsor Alfredo, who sends them to the address of his own sponsor, Ken Whitman. He tells Holmes and Watson that his daughter Eva was drugged and raped by a man named Brent Garvey, and though Garvey was subsequently jailed, Whitman has recently received a video recording of the incident along with a blackmail demand.

Tracing the blackmailer, Charles Augustus Milverton, proves to be an easy task, but when Holmes breaks into his Staten Island home to recover the videos, he sees Milverton shot dead by a masked man, who subsequently removes the body.

Holmes contacts Gregson, but is anxious that Milverton's accomplice, who is mentioned in the demand sent to Whitman, should continue to believe the blackmailer is dead, for fear that he might release incriminating material on the web.

Suspecting that the imprisoned Brent Garvey might be that accomplice, Holmes questions the rapist. But Garvey is another of Milverton's victims, and knows nothing of any other blackmail material.

Alfredo spots attorney Duke Landers attempting to enter Milverton's home. When questioned by Holmes and Watson, Landers reluctantly admits knowing the blackmailer and is aware of the existence of an accomplice, but insists that he was simply a supplier of incriminating material.

Examining Milverton's ledger, Holmes sees that regular payments were made to someone listed as Henry 8, and suspects that the codename refers to one of Landers' clients, Abraham Zellner. Further investigation reveals that the name Zellner is another pseudonym.

Another of Milverton's victims, Anthony Pistone, is arrested attempting to dispose of the blackmailer's body. He confesses to the murder. The world will now know Milverton is dead. When all seems lost, Whitman receives a new blackmail demand, sent by Henry 8.

Holmes finally identifies Abaraham Zellner as Stuart Bloom. He and Watson go to confront Bloom, but instead discover his rotting corpse. The evidence suggests that Bloom was killed by Milverton, so who has the blackmail material now?

When Milverton's autopsy report comes in, Holmes notes that Anthony Pistone stamped on the blackmailer's head, obliterating existing scars, scars that match Pistone's ring. It turns out that he had given Milverton a severe beating on an earlier occasion, at which time Pistone demanded a piece of his operation. Milverton's laptop is discovered in the possession of Pistone's brother, proving his guilt.

The best and the wisest man: Holmes is first seen touching up his tattoos. He claims he's ambidextrous, something most of us would give our right arm to be. He hates cats (does he have allergies, like Stephen King's depiction of the detective in his pastiche *The Doctor's Case*?), considers blackmailers, in some respects, more despicable than murderers, and takes pleasure in seeing the beating Brent Garvey has received in prison. From this point on in the series, he largely dispenses with his grungy look in favour of smart suits and waistcoats.

I am lost without my Boswell: Having absorbed several volumes on handwriting analysis, Joan has no difficulty in identifying Duke Landers' law licence as a forgery. She's just about ready for her spinoff: *Joan Watson - The Crime Doctor*!

The efficiency of our detective police force: Gregson is far from amused at being asked to watch the video of Eva Whitman's rape without any explanation from Holmes. He has more than one daughter. He thinks Blum might have been murdered by Anthony Pistone.

Bell's input is minor, but compared to his contribution to the next episode, it's positively gargantuan.

There is a strong family resemblance about misdeeds: This is the first episode to draw its plot – at least in part – from a Canonical adventure. In *Charles Augustus Milverton*, Holmes and Watson are employed by a victim of "the worst man in London." They break into his home in order to retrieve an incriminating letter, and witness the blackmailer being shot dead by a masked woman. Robert Hardy played Milverton in the massively overlong Jeremy Brett version of this tale, *The Master Blackmailer*. The makers of the BBC's *Sherlock* have promised their own take on the story in Season Three, in which the villain's surname has become Magnussen.

A seven-per-cent solution: As he adds embellishments to his tattoos, Holmes observes "It's the only needle these arms see nowadays."

He's heading for his sober anniversary, at which time he'll be presented with a one-year chip. He thinks the idea infantile: "It is absurd to measure sobriety in units of time – it is a state of being. One is either in it or out of it." He orders a large number of chips online, in order, he claims, to see what all the fuss is about, and tells Alfredo that he can't accept a chip because he feels it commemorates "the end of a period of great failure." Finally, he tearfully confesses to Joan that he relapsed just after entering Hemdale – it isn't actually his anniversary. He still refuses to accept a sobriety chip, so Joan presents him with a framed copy of the final stanza of Robert Frost's famous *Stopping by Woods on a Snowy Evening*.

He challenges Watson to smell his breath and confirm that he hasn't been drinking.

A certain unexpected vein of pawky humour: In the absence of a sensory deprivation chamber, Holmes proposes attempting to regress Alfredo by locking him in the trunk of his car. Luckily, Joan recognises the description of the man he saw at Milverton's home as Duke Landers before the situation becomes Tarantino-esque.

Holmes calls the garishly-coloured sobriety chips "more appropriate to a successful first year as a Vegas showgirl."

When Joan describes Zellner as heavyset, he responds: "Orson Welles was heavyset; Abraham Zellner could pull small moons out of orbit."

Holmes: "Captain, what is the first thing that comes to mind when I say Henry VIII?" Gregson: "Herman's Hermits?"

As in *Flight Risk*, Holmes sits in Watson's bedroom,

waiting for her to wake up. It's a rather a creepy habit, and she needs to talk to him about it.

This episode follows a brief break in the run, and from now until the finale, the promos become quite serious in tone.

Holmes' rather blunt but factual accusation, "You're a liar... who lies," shows up in the promo for Season Two, for some reason.

My head is in a whirl: For the third time this season, Holmes and Watson are permitted to remove evidence from a house where a murder has just been committed – this week, it's Milverton's ledger. Are crime scenes the equivalent of garage sales in New York?

"I can't recall when I was so thankful for the essential avarice of the human condition." Like the James Bond film *The Living Daylights*, the original literary source serves as a prologue for an entirely new adventure. The sobriety chip storyline doesn't really add up to much, but Miller gives it his all, and is one of the very few Holmeses to cry onscreen, along with Nicol Williamson, Christopher Plummer and Jeremy Brett.

1X21: A Landmark Story
US Airdate: 2 May 2013

Writer: Corrine Brinkerhoff
Director: Peter Werner

Guest Cast: Roger Aaron Brown (John Douglas); Byron Jennings (Phillip Van Der Hoff); F Murray Abraham (Daniel Gottlieb); Berto Colon (Will); Helen Coxe (Hillary Taggart); Tony F DeVito (Convict #1); Aaron Berg (Convict #2); Mark DiConzo (Uniformed Cop); Laurence Lau (Robert Baumann): Morgan Weed (The Girl With Rainbow Hair); Bryan A Miranda (Sikh With Turban); Carl Ducena (NYPD Officer)*

*Uncredited

Plot: Phillip Van Der Hoff is killed in a most unusual manner by an urbane killer who uses a laptop to tamper with his pacemaker unless he agrees to cast a vote concerning a particular property in New York. After voting as he is instructed, Van Der Hoff is killed anyway.

The imprisoned Sebastian Moran sees the news report about the death and demands to talk to Holmes – Van Der Hoff was to have been his next target, had he not been captured.

Examining the corpse, Holmes and Watson discover the imaginative means of murder, and subsequently the motive – Van Der Hoff and others were members of New York's Landmark Protection council, debating the status of the famous Taggart Speakeasy Museum. Most of those who changed their votes willingly were bribed with the promise of a home renovation, courtesy of skyscraper builder Robert Baumann, who is killed by a falling air conditioning unit before he can be questioned.

It appears that someone has taken over Moran's post as Moriarty's chief assassin, someone who specializes in committing murders that appear to be accidents.

Holmes decides that Hillary Taggart, last surviving relative of the mobster who owned the speakeasy during the prohibition era, will be the next target and that the best way to save her life is to determine how she is to be killed.

As he and Watson watch Hillary jog, the detective is distracted by the buzzing of an Africanized honey bee. Joan has spotted that Hillary wears a medic alert bracelet. The creative killer is planning to have her attacked by "an army of bee assassins."

Staking out the hive, Holmes stuns the killer, Daniel Gottlieb, and takes him back to the brownstone. Gottlieb, like Moran, receives encrypted texts from Moriarty. Under duress, he makes an appointment with his employer.

Watson and Holmes watch the restaurant where Gottlieb's contact has arranged to meet, and get a photo of the man, John Douglas. Holmes tracks Douglas to his hotel room, but he is killed by a marksman before he can talk.

Another coded message is sent to Gottlieb's phone. When he insists he can't translate it, Holmes takes the message to Moran. He, too, claims it is meaningless. The detective eventually cracks the code, a threat to the life of Moran's sister. Holmes is too late to prevent Moran's suicide attempt. As he berates himself, Gottlieb's phone rings again – the caller is an Englishmen who identifies himself as Moriarty. "I believe we're overdue for a chat..."

The best and the wisest man: Holmes dislocates his own shoulder in an attempt to get out of a straightjacket. His doll abuse continues – he burns Barbie's boyfriend Ken at the stake to symbolise an ongoing dispute he has with a theologist concerning Galileo. He considers Watson "an interesting project."

I am lost without my Boswell: Watson twice gets to show off her medical abilities in this episode. She resets Holmes' dislocated shoulder, and later, much against her will, she performs an illicit autopsy on Phillip Van Der Hoff (Well, we were all young once, weren't we?).

The efficiency of our detective police force: Gregson doubts that Holmes is telling the truth about what occurred when he spoke to Moran. If he'd pressed his consultant for an answer, John Douglas might not have been killed, too (assuming that Moran is indeed dead).
    Bell is seen interrogating Gottlieb, but has no dialogue.

There is a strong family resemblance about misdeeds: Holmes says that he once broke into a funeral parlour during *The Problem of Thor Bridge* (which Miller pronounces "Tor").
    John Douglas shares his name with the victim in *The Valley of Fear*, whose death is arranged by Moriarty. As a target or a as a minion, he still winds up dead.
    "Some people without possessing genius have a remarkable knack for stimulating it," Holmes remarks, quoting his sentiments in the first chapter of *The Hound of the Baskervilles*. Joan considers it both an insult and a boast. Who can blame her? The same back-handed compliment is given in *Sherlock*'s *The Hounds of Baskerville*.

I have never loved: There's mention of Irene Adler, and Holmes' intentions regarding her killer.

A seven-per-cent solution: Holmes likens his intent

regarding violence towards Gottlieb to his actions should he discover a syringe filled with heroin – unknowable.

Gottlieb was arranging an accidental overdose for Holmes in London before being advised by Moriarty that the hit was cancelled.

Joan apologises to Holmes after saying she needs a drink.

A certain unexpected vein of pawky humour: Joan critiques Holmes' attempts at dissection. When she takes over, he praises her skill. "I am dissecting a body in the middle of the night," she points out, "we are not having a moment!"

The funniest scene in the entire series occurs when, immediately after Joan says an air conditioning unit could not possibly be dropped onto a moving target, she is seen folding her clothes in the brownstone... as an air conditioner flies past the window.

My head is in a whirl: Holmes mispronounces jazz legend Bix Beiderbecke's surname (it's a safe bet that the villain in this episode is named after Danny Gottlieb, another jazz musician).

Once again, Holmes keeps hold of a vital piece of evidence with the blessing of the NYPD. Wouldn't they want to examine Gottlieb's phone?

Is Roger Aaron Brown being dubbed? He sounds suspiciously like the actor Colin Salmon.

Moriarty, it seems, must own the land on which the Taggart Speakeasy stands – even if intermediaries are involved, it seems like a profitable avenue of investigation, but Holmes never even considers looking into it.

"We're obviously pursuing a lively intellect." This is the beginning of a four-episode run that will resolve the issues with Moriarty and the murder of Irene Adler. F Murray Abraham is so striking a presence that for the early portion of the episode, it appears that he might actually *be* Moriarty. Vinnie Jones' Moran is just plain terrifying, killing a prison guard who might have overheard his conversation with Holmes. His own suicide attempt, ramming his head repeatedly into a mirror is no less horrific. Gregson reports in the final scene that Moran is not expected to survive, but his fate is still left up in the air (probably in case the writers decide to bring Vinnie back). As a point of trivia, it's a pretty safe bet that this is the first use of the word "dildo" in a Holmesian pastiche.

1X22: Risk Management
US Airdate: 9 May 2013

Writer: Liz Friedman
Story: Liz Friedman & Robert Doherty
Director: Adam Davidson

Guest Cast: J C MacKenzie (Daren Sutter); Francie Swift (Katie Sutter); Stephanie Kurtzuber (Eileen Rourke); Sean Dougherty (Detective); Con Horgan (Wallace Rourke); Perri Lauren (Leah Sutter); Adam Godley (British Man: Voice)*

*Uncredited

Plot: To Holmes' surprise, Moriarty wants to hire him to investigate the murder of mechanic Wallace Rourke, killed in Brooklyn the previous December. In return for his services, Holmes will receive the answers he has been seeking concerning Irene's murder.

Rourke's widow Eileen knows of no-one named Moriarty, but mentions that her husband believed he was being followed in the weeks leading up to his death.

Examining his belongings, Holmes finds evidence that Wallace Rourke was being tracked via his cellphone. That clue takes them to the offices of upscale detective agency Sutter Risk Management. Daren Sutter admits that his company were conducting surveillance on Wallace Rourke for a client, but Holmes is convinced that there is no client, and that Sutter was therefore having Rourke followed for some personal reason.

Sutter's autobiography mentions the murder twenty years earlier of his sister Leah by a home invader who matches Rourke's description. It seems likely that Moriarty wishes to see Sutter Risk Management brought down by discrediting its head. Meeting privately, Holmes advises Daren Sutter that his offices are probably bugged. Hours later, Sutter walks into the police station and confesses to Rourke's murder. But the case is far from over - Moriarty phones Holmes and informs him that Rourke was in Saudi Arabia at the time of Leah Sutter's murder. It appears that her brother killed the wrong man.

Watson speaks to Sutter's wife, Kate, who tells Joan that she met Daren at a candlelight vigil for his late sister. Later, Watson realises that Kate lied to her. She knew Daren before the murder. In fact, Kate – married to another man at the time - was having an affair with Daren. She was the one who found Leah's body, not Daren. He claimed to have seen the killer to protect Kate. Years later, when Daren had grown so despondent he was contemplating suicide, Kate set Rourke up by insisting to her husband that he was the man she saw on the night of Leah's murder.

After Holmes breaks the news to Sutter, Moriarty texts him an address in Douglastown where the answers he seeks can be found. Joan meets him there, and they enter the house together. It seems abandoned at first, but they are drawn to classical music coming from the conservatory. There, they find paintings in various stages of completion, and working at an easel... Irene Adler.

The best and the wisest man: Holmes usually considers optimism a sign of stupidity, but not in Irene's case. He carries a device to sweep for electronic bugs – presumably, he's used it to check the brownstone, given Moriarty's renewed interest in him. He considers himself a scarred man, and there is the implication that he almost envies Sutter for taking revenge upon his tormentor. Frustrated at Moriarty's failure to contact him, he kicks a football repeatedly across the living room, much to Joan's annoyance. When she suggests that Wallace Rourke's lack of bank activity twenty years earlier might be because his mother paid for everything, he call it "a relationship that is not unheard of," presumably referring to his own arrangement with his father. He considers fear an unproductive filter through which to view the world.

I am lost without my Boswell: Joan is wary of Holmes' involvement in the Rourke investigation, concerned that it might be a trap. She thinks – correctly – that Gregson is trying to get rid of her by arranging a sobriety counselling job for her. She is somewhat troubled about her own safety, despite Holmes' assurance that he will never allow any harm to befall her. She reaches the solution to the Sutter case from her own concern for Holmes' well-being, and her wish that she could somehow arrange matters in order to restore his peace of mind. Convinced that Holmes will try to ditch him, she tracks him via Gottlieb's phone and meets him at the gates of the Douglastown house. She feels she deserves answers as much as Holmes.

The efficiency of our detective police force: Gregson is at his most affable early on in this episode. He asks her to act as sober companion to the daughter of his friend Eddie. In fact, he's trying to put her out of harm's (and Holmes') way. "Guys like him," he warns her, "they walk between the raindrops. They don't get wet. People like you do." It's the first time he addresses her as "Joan" rather than "Ms Watson." He's been a cop for thirty years.

   Bell reports Sutter's arrival at the station. And that's his sole contribution to this episode.

There is a strong family resemblance about misdeeds: Moriarty repeats Holmes' own description of him from *The Final Problem*: "Consider me a spider - I sit motionless at the centre of my web. That web has a thousand radiations, and I know well every quiver of each of them. I do little myself, I only plan. My agents are numerous and splendidly organised. If there is a crime to be done, a paper to be abstracted, a house to be rifled, a man to be removed, the word is passed to me, the matter is planned and carried out."

Holmes, likewise, quotes Watson's opening paragraph from *A Scandal in Bohemia* when recalling Irene: "She was, to me, *the* woman. To me, she eclipsed and predominated the whole of her gender."

He mentions his singlestick skills to Daren Sutter.

I have never loved: Holmes likens Moriarty to a pimp – the subject of prostitution seems never far from his mind. Tellingly, he also likens Joan to a wife (no sex and a lot of arguments – that does sound like a wife).

He describes Irene as "difficult to explain – and I mean that as a compliment." He held the fact that she was American against her only briefly and considered her an exquisite painter and lover. She was the only woman he ever loved.

Joan draws a gun/penis comparison in her conversation with Gregson.

A seven-per-cent solution: Astonishingly, given that Moriarty's involvement brings Holmes' feeling about Irene and her apparent murder to the fore, the subject of his addiction is never raised.

A certain unexpected vein of pawky humour: Holmes wakes a snoozing Joan up by flicking a light on and off in her face. "Oh good, you're awake."

When she enters the bathroom as he's brushing his teeth, he tells her: "If you want to use the toilet, I'll just turn away. You didn't have asparagus last night, did you?"

My head is in a whirl: Holmes still has Gottlieb's phone. The police really don't want that, especially since a text sent on it resulted in the (probable) death of Sebastian Moran?

"Most puzzles I see from the outside – it gives me a certain clarity. I am right in the centre of this one, it has blurred my vision to say the least." The idea of someone setting up an ideal victim is one that has been used several times before in *Elementary*, notably in the pilot episode and *Lesser Evils*, but it is the depth of Daren Sutter's passion that sets this story apart. Too many episodes of late have been missing the human factor, but this one has it in spades. Irene's reappearance may not have been a surprise to anyone with access to the internet, but Jonny Lee Miller's distress and Lucy Liu's evident concern sell the drama of the moment brilliantly.

1X23: The Woman
US Airdate: 16 May 2013

Writers: Robert Doherty & Craig Sweeny
Director: Seith Mann

Guest Cast: John Bedford Lloyd (Lieutenant); Lucas Caleb Rooney (Duane Proctor); Christopher McCann (Dr Del Santo); Frank Deal (Detective Mike Muldoon); Henry Hodges (Student); David Boston (Hospital Patient)*

*Uncredited

Plot: In a flashback, we see Holmes first meeting with Irene in London. Investigating a forgery case, he's been referred to her by a Mr Kirby of the British Museum, who considers Irene his top restorer. Holmes realises that she has an original Breughel on her wall, having returned her copy to the Belgian National Museum. This, oddly, proves to be the beginning of their relationship. "I appreciate your efforts to keep the vulgarities of the modern era at bay," he tells her. As their relationship deepens, she begins work on a painting she keeps behind a locked door. When Holmes goes to her place to view the finished work, he finds a pool of blood and a message from the serial killer known as M.

In 2013, Irene is in hospital, claiming to have been kept in the Douglastown house by a masked man named Mr Stapleton. Her doctor diagnoses a case of post-traumatic stress. She is brought back to the brownstone to stay. Joan's deductions at the Douglastown prison lead to the cops to a Dwayne Proctor, who bought Irene's paint supplies. But Dwayne has been making the purchases on behalf of his brother Isaac, a former CIA interrogator, who shoots a cop while making his escape. On the run from the cops, Isaac betrays the Moriarty organisation and grows determined to kill Holmes.

When the security of the brownstone is breached, Holmes realises he must send Irene away until Moriarty can be captured. She agrees to do so only if he accompanies her. As they prepare to leave, he notices that one of Irene's birthmarks has been surgically removed. He accuses her of working for Moriarty. In a fury, she walks out on him.

Holmes returns to the brownstone and is shot by Proctor, who admits to being the sniper who murdered John Douglas. Before he can finish off Holmes, though, Proctor is killed by Moriarty, whose true identity is revealed at last... it's Irene.

The best and the wisest man: Holmes doesn't propose investigating Irene's abduction and incarceration, preferring instead to look after his lost love. On their second date, he took her on a tour of the tunnels underneath Camden Market. He says that he was once required to make an extensive study of London's catacombs. With the help of a few sticks of dynamite, he discovered a quarter-of-a-mile long Roman canal. He received a garage in payment for a job he did shortly after his arrival in New York. He decided to keep it as a safe house. It's presumably wishful thinking on Holmes' part that Watson might dismantle Moriarty's empire while he and Irene are on the run.

I am lost without my Boswell: Watson finds herself working on Irene's case without Holmes' assistance, but Bell considers the experience very similar. Her recent training assignments concerned forged artwork and she's able to put the knowledge to good use. She tells Holmes that by fleeing with Irene, he's doing just what Moriarty wants – she doesn't know how right she is.

The efficiency of our detective police force: Gregson is doubtful about the existence of Moriarty. He and Bell have a good deal to do this episode, following up leads relating to the Irene affair, and only narrowly missing out on an action sequence when Isaac Proctor makes his escape. Holmes trusts both men implicitly.

There is a strong family resemblance about misdeeds: In the flashbacks, Irene makes a passing reference to the Afghan War, the conflict in which the Canonical Watson was injured, resulting in his return to London and first encounter with Sherlock Holmes.

Her non-existent captor "Mr Stapleton" is named after the culprit in *The Hound of the Baskervilles*.

Holmes says, "A man should know when he's beaten," which might or might not be a veiled reference to Irene Adler's website masthead in the *Sherlock* episode *A Scandal in Belgravia*.

I have never loved: Irene proclaims Holmes beautiful on their first meeting. Their banter results in a "sexual marathon." Holmes is seen making notes on the Moran case immediately after making love. Irene wonders if she's become no more than a piece of exercise equipment to him. When she moves into the brownstone, he tells her that she's the only woman with whom he ever empathised.

A seven-per-cent solution: Holmes thinks Moriarty stage-managed Irene's "death" in order to push him into heroin addiction. Joan considers her dramatic reappearance a trigger.

He admits to dabbling with narcotics during their

relationship. "I'm sober now; I'll always be an addict."

A certain unexpected vein of pawky humour: As Bell questions Dwayne Proctor about his brother Isaac, he asks: "Did he ever mention a guy named Moriarty?" Dwayne replies: "We went to high school with a guy named Maury Goldberg."

My head is in a whirl: Holmes wonders where the blood at the scene of Irene's murder came from. We never find out.
"I've never consulted without you before," says Joan. Isn't that just what she did in *Déjà Vu All Over Again*, just a few episodes ago?
In the London flashbacks, Holmes refers to "spelunkers" when an Englishman would say "potholers."
Why does the fact that Irene has had a mole removed automatically mean that she's working for Moriarty? If, as Holmes, suggests, it was pre-cancerous, this seems like an eminently sensible thing for a captor with limitless resources to do – what use is a dead hostage?
It's incredibly convenient that Watson has been studying art forgery just when that knowledge becomes of practical use.
During the scene in which Proctor and his fellow minions discuss Moriarty, everybody goes out of their way not to say "he," tipping us off that the Napoleon of Crime is actually female.
And what makes Proctor so special that he should be in on the secret, when not even Moran or Gottlieb were ever permitted to meet their employer? Considering his skills as a marksman, Proctor seems a closer match to the Canonical Moran than the brutish assassin seen in this series.

"It's weird to see him walk away from a case." Irene is Moriarty? For some, it's as horrific a notion as, say, Holmes recovering from substance addiction in 21st Century New York. But in the continuity of *Elementary*, as established over the previous 22 episodes, it works. This episode and *Heroine* were originally screened in the US as a double-length season finale. The recreation of London is pretty well done, and it's odd to have entire scenes that don't feature Holmes, Watson, or even our two favourite cops, a sure sign that something out of the ordinary is going on.

1X24: Heroine
US Airdate: 16 May 2013

Writers: Robert Doherty & Craig Sweeny
Director: John Polson

Guest Cast: Dominic Fumusa (Jordan Conroy); Michael Aronov (Andrej Bacera); Austin Lysy (Chad Lerberg); Arnold Vosloo (Christos Theophilus); Justine Cotsonas (Jovana Bacera); Karen Ludwig (Melanie Waters); Kevyn Morrow (ND Detective); Raquel Toro (Alethea Lerberg)*

*Uncredited

Plot: Speaking with an English accent, Moriarty tells Holmes that she caused his downfall through drug addiction after he foiled a series of assassinations in London. Her existence as Irene Adler was merely an experiment. Holmes senses that he must be close to uncovering one of her schemes in New York, which is why she chose to reappear. She leaves him alive, but wounded.

At the morgue, Holmes finds the modified cellphones of the minions killed by Isaac Proctor. Decoding a text on one of the phones, he finds that Greek tycoon and former smuggler Christos Theophilus is somehow connected to Moriarty's plot.

Watching the unloading of one of his vessels, the cops spot Theophilus himself, and find that he has been smuggling endangered animals. They confirm this by interviewing Theophilus' son-in-law Chad Lerberg at his home, where Holmes concludes that the tycoon's daughter Alethea has been kidnapped. Moriarty blackmails Theophilus into murdering Macedonian diplomat Andrej Bacera.

Joan is waylaid by Moriarty, who is puzzled by her role in Holmes' life. She can only imagine that Joan is some sort of mascot for him. Joan concludes that Moriarty is afraid of Holmes.

Staying awake all night, Holmes works out Moriarty's plan: she has purchased an enormous position in the soon-to-be outmoded Macedonian currency, the dinar. The assassination of Andrej Bacera will prevent the country joining the EU and switching to the Euro, thus netting Moriarty a billion dollars.

The cops are too late to prevent Theophilus from killing Bacera and his wife before being shot dead himself by Bacera's bodyguard Conroy, another of Moriarty's agents.

In immense pain, and confounded at every turn, Holmes is close to losing control. Joan convinces him that he must let Moriarty win. After Holmes returns to the brownstone, Bell – who is on guard duty – receives a call from Gregson alerting him to a recent drug store robbery committed by a man matching Holmes' description. Kicking down the bathroom door, the cop finds Sherlock on the floor, a syringe by his side, having apparently overdosed.

Holmes is visited in hospital by Moriarty. She offers to take him out of the country. Holmes tells her that they both made the mistake of falling in love – her own condition was diagnosed by his "mascot." Moriarty couldn't bring herself to kill Holmes because of her feelings for him. His overdose was a fake – the police are waiting at the door.

The series ends with Holmes and Watson on the roof of the brownstone – Moriarty has been arrested and her dinars confiscated. The bee Holmes received from Gerald Lydon in *Possibility Two* has mated. The two friends sit and watch the birth of a new species, which Holmes has named *Euglassia Watsonia*.

The best and the wisest man: Holmes claims that

discovering the truth about Irene is quite liberating, and that he now sees with perfect clarity. Of course, he is in considerable emotional pain throughout the episode, as well as suffering physical pain resulting from Proctor's attempt on his life. He considers narwhals "lovely creatures." During the all-nighter he requires to work out Moriarty's scheme, he keeps himself awake by slamming his hand into his wound.

I am lost without my Boswell: Watson sews up Holmes' bullet wound. She agrees to to accompany him so long as she is permitted to tend to his injury. Joan gets a call from her brother telling her that their mother has suffered a fall and is in Chandler Memorial Hospital (the scene of *Lesser Evils*). Moriarty becomes the second person in the show to address her as "my dear Watson." Two of her cousins wanted to name their child Henry, resulting in a fraught Thanksgiving dinner.

The efficiency of our detective police force: Gregson is still having difficulty with the whole "criminal mastermind" thing. He attempts to warn Conroy about the assassination attempt, not realising that the bodyguard is in on the plot.

While on a stakeout, Bell tries to relate to Holmes. Surprisingly, it goes quite well. He does some pretty sterling work concerning the e-mail account opened by Moriarty in order to contact Theophilus. Despite the events of *You do it to Yourself*, it's still not clear whether Bell knows about Holmes' addiction. For some reason, Gregson doesn't let him in on the fake overdose ploy. Surely he trusts Bell, so does he think the uniformed cops might be on Moriarty's payroll?

There is a strong family resemblance about misdeeds:

Having Watson drawn away with a message concerning a sick woman is the ruse Moriarty employs in *The Final Problem* (and that *Sherlock's* Moriarty employs in *The Reichenbach Fall*). In the Canonical story, it's so that Watson will not be on hand to intervene as Holmes and his arch-enemy fight to the death. Here, it's because Moriarty wishes to speak to Joan privately.

She boasts that she has "plotted exactly seven murders that were carried out in crowded restaurants." The recent Robert Downey Jr sequel *Sherlock Holmes: A Game of Shadows* begins with Moriarty killing a woman in a crowded restaurant. That woman was *the* woman, Irene Adler. In this story, Irene *is* Moriarty.

I have never loved: With the revelation of Irene's true identity, love turns to... well... "I have about as much in common with you as I do a dung beetle," Holmes tells her.

During their meeting, Moriarty asks Joan if she wants to sleep with Holmes. She evades the question. Perhaps that's what tips Watson off to the nature of Moriarty's own feelings for Sherlock.

A seven-per-cent solution: Holmes doesn't want any non-addictive painkillers: "How good can they be if they're non-addictive?"

Joan thinks that "marinating in his own mistakes" might push him over the edge into relapse.

He is tempted by a bottle of Vicodin in Alethea Lerberg's home, but doesn't take it because he knows how disappointed Joan would be in him.

A certain unexpected vein of pawky humour: When checking the pain levels after he's been shot, Joan asks Holmes to rate his discomfort on a scale of 1 to 10. "Pi," is his response.

The flick of the head he gives when leading Joan to his wall of evidence prior to delivering a lecture on the dinar is absolutely priceless.

My head is in a whirl: Watson questions the likelihood of Holmes having a Macedonian dinar "just lying around." I do, too.

Shouldn't someone be keeping Theophilus under surveillance? If they had, he might not have been able to keep his appointment with Moriarty and receive the gun he uses to kill Andrej and his wife Jovana. Also, shouldn't a former criminal be able to lay his hands on a gun of his own without too much difficulty?

For such a complex plan, Moriarty has certainly left a lot of things 'til the last minute – Holmes says she only bought into the dinar 48 hours earlier.

Is there really all that much in Moriarty's recorded conversation with Holmes in the hospital that might result in a conviction? She doesn't actually admit to anything!

"I have reserves of creativity I haven't even begun to tap." Sherlock Holmes and Joan Watson have come a long way since their first meeting. Both were, in their own way, damaged, and though their working relationship has helped them both to heal, there is still some way to go. There are questions that have yet to be resolved. Will Moriarty go to jail, and even if she does, is that the end of her criminal empire? Is Moran dead? If not, what will he do and to whom when he comes round? Holmes has managed to remain clean for the entire season, but as he says in *The Woman*, he'll always be an addict. What of Joan's future? Is it tied to Holmes' for the remainder of their lives? There's plenty of material for Season Two of *Elementary*. But for now, let's just leave them both, sitting on the brownstone roof, watching the bees as the sun sets behind them. They've earned it.

THE FUTURE

The success of both series means that further episodes are guaranteed – *Sherlock* has been renewed for a further two seasons. As before, Season Three is made of up a trio of episodes: *The Empty Hearse* by Mark Gatiss, *The Sign of Three* by Steve Thompson and *His Last Vow* by Steven Moffat. Watson's bride Mary Morstan will appear, played by Martin Freeman's real-life partner Amanda Abbington. The final episode will feature *Sherlock'*s interpretation of "the worst man in London," media baron Charles Augusts Magnussen, as portrayed by Lars Mikkelsen.

At the time of writing, Season Two of *Elementary* has yet to air, but as has been well-recorded elsewhere, the first episode, *Step Nine*, takes place in London, and given that shooting there took place at the height of a heatwave, might give American viewers a very different impression of the British climate. The ninth step of the AA program for recovering addicts, by the way, is to make amends to those the addict may have harmed, which gives some indication of what may occur. Sean Pertwee will play Inspector Gareth Lestrade (pronounced "Lestrarde" again) and Rhys Ifans is brother Mycroft, whom Sherlock addresses as "Fatty." The plot of this first episode will involve gossip-monger Langdale Pike, mentioned but unseen in *The Three Gables*. A DCI Hopkins (Tim McMullen), named after the Canon's Stanley Hopkins will also feature in some way. Perhaps most importantly, the writers have revealed via Twitter that the standout character of Season One, Clyde the Tortoise, will reappear.

All this, and the possibility of a third Victorian-era movie starring Robert Downey Jr and Jude Law? The near-future for Sherlock Holmes appears very bright, and I, for one, can't get enough of it.

ABOUT THE AUTHOR

Matthew J Elliott is a writer and dramatist whose articles, fiction and reviews have appeared in the magazines *SHERLOCK*, *Sherlock Holmes Mystery Magazine*, *Total DVD* and *Scarlet Street*.

For the radio, he has scripted episodes of *The Further Adventures of Sherlock Holmes*, *The Classic Adventures of Sherlock Holmes*, *Jeeves and Wooster*, *Wrath of the Titans*, *Logan's Run: Aftermath*, *Fangoria's Dreadtime Stories*, *Raffles the Gentleman Thief*, *The Twilight Zone*, *The Father Brown Mysteries*, *Kincaid the Strangeseeker*, *The Adventures of Harry Nile*, *The Thinking Machine*, *The Perry Mason Radio Dramas*, *Vincent Price Presents*, *Fantom House of Horrors*, *Allan Quatermain*, *The War of the Worlds*, *The Prince and the Pauper* and the Audie Award-nominated *New Adventures of Mickey Spillane's Mike Hammer*. He is the creator of *The Hilary Caine Mysteries*, which first aired in 2005.

His stage play *An Evening With Jeeves and Wooster* was performed at the Palace Theatre, Grapevine, Texas in 2007.

He is the author of *Sherlock Holmes on the Air* (2012) and *Sherlock Holmes in Pursuit* (2013), both published by MX and *Lost in Time and Space: An Unofficial Guide to the Uncharted Journeys of Doctor Who* (Hasslein Books, 20014). He has also contributed to the Sherlockian short story volumes *The Game's Afoot*, *Curious Incidents 2* and *Gaslight Grimoire*. His Sherlock Holmes story *Art in the Blood* appeared in *The Mammoth Book of Best British Crime 8* in the UK, and *The Mammoth Book of Best British Crime 8* in the US. He is the editor of the collections *The Whisperer in Darkness*, *The Horror in the Museum*, *The Haunter of the Dark* and *The Lurking Fear* by H P Lovecraft, *The Right Hand of Doom* and *The*

Haunter of the Ring by Robert E Howard, and *A Charlie Chan Omnibus* by Earl Derr Biggers.

Matthew is probably best-known as a writer/performer on RiffTrax.com, the online comedy experience from the makers of cult sci-fi TV series *Mystery Science Theater 3000* (*MST3K* to the initiated). He also writes comic books for Bluewater.

If the makers of *Elementary* are reading this, he's totally available for any spinoff novels.

He lives in the North-West of England with his wife and daughter.

Also from MX Publishing

MX Publishing is the world's largest specialist Sherlock Holmes publisher, with over a hundred titles and fifty authors creating the latest in Sherlock Holmes fiction and non-fiction. From traditional short stories and novels to travel guides and quiz books, MX Publishing cater for all Holmes fans. The collection includes leading titles such as *Benedict Cumberbatch In Transition* and *The Norwood Author* the winner of the 2011 Howlett Award (Sherlock Holmes Book of the Year). MX Publishing also has one of the largest communities of Holmes fans on Facebook with regular contributions from dozens of authors.

www.ingramcontent.com/pod-product-compliance
Lightning Source LLC
Chambersburg PA
CBHW071704090426
42738CB00009B/1658